THE
EDGAR CAYCE
HANDBOOK
FOR
CREATING
YOUR FUTURE

**Mark Thurston, Ph.D.,
and Christopher Fazel**

BALLANTINE BOOKS • NEW YORK

Copyright © 1992 by Mark Thurston, Ph.D., and Christopher Fazel

All rights reserved under International and Pan-American Copyright Conventions. Published in the United States of America by Ballantine Books, a division of Random House, Inc., New York, and simultaneously in Canada by Random House of Canada Limited, Toronto.

Grateful acknowledgment is made to the following for permission to reprint previously published material:
Doubleday: Excerpt from THE DIARY OF A YOUNG GIRL by Anne Frank. Reprinted by permission of Doubleday, a division of Bantam, Doubleday, Dell Publishing Group, Inc.
Macmillan Publishing Company: Excerpt from INSIDE THE THIRD REICH by Albert Speer. Copyright © 1969 by Verlag Ullstein GMbH. Translation copyright © 1970 by Macmillan Publishing Company. Reprinted by permission of Macmillan Publishing Company.

Library of Congress Catalog Card Number: 91-92389

ISBN 0-345-36467-8

Printed in Canada

First Ballantine Books Edition: July 1992

Cover photo by the Uniphoto Picture Agency

Praise for
THE EDGAR CAYCE HANDBOOK

"Mark Thurston and Christopher Fazel have done a commendable job in their new book. With the increase in interest in spiritual experiences which our society has seen over the past two decades, it is nice to have a convenient guidebook for the personal exploration and practical use of altered states of awareness."

RAYMOND A. MOODY, JR.
Author of *Life after Life*
and *The Light Beyond*

"The phenomenon of Edgar Cayce's psychic powers is well known; his far more important qualities of compassion and wisdom are not as widely appreciated. This book does a great service by making Cayce's practical spirituality accessible to and usable for all of us."

JACOB NEEDLEMAN
Author of *Money and the Meaning of Life*

"The material in Thurston and Fazel's book is a remarkable application of Edgar Cayce's ideas and concepts to the turbulence typically encountered today in our relationships, our work, and our spiritual development."

STANLEY KRIPPNER, PH. D.

"The twenty-four principles outlined in this book offer a complete guide to living a meaningful, joyous life. I highly recommend it."

C. NORMAN SHEALY, M.D., PH.D.
Founding President
American Holistic Medical Association

Also by Mark Thurston:

Soul Purpose: Discovering and Fulfilling Your Destiny
Dreams: Tonight's Answers for Tomorrow's Questions
Paradox of Power
The Inner Power of Silence
Edgar Cayce Predicts
Discovering Your Soul's Purpose
How to Interpret Your Dreams
Understand and Develop Your ESP
Experiments in Practical Spirituality
Experiments in a Search for God
Meditation and the Mind of Man (coauthor)

Dedication

To our wives, Mary Elizabeth and Sharon,
whose love and support
make creating our futures a joy.

Table of Contents

Acknowledgments

We wish to thank those many individuals who have helped us understand and interpret the rich legacy of material left by Edgar Cayce. Among our valued teachers have been Hugh Lynn Cayce, Harmon Bro, Nell Clairmonte, Richard Drummond, and Herbert Puryear.

We also want to thank our editor at Ballantine, Cheryl Woodruff. Her enthusiasm for this project has been just the sort of support that every author hopes for.

Introduction

The story of Edgar Cayce's life is exceptional in its simplicity. His strongest motives were caring about people and wanting to help. Out of that impulse came remarkable abilities—talents that were destined to make him more famous decades after his death than he was in his own time.

At the age of twenty-one, this gentle, unassuming man discovered by accident that he could intuitively tap sources of knowledge far beyond his eighth-grade education. A compassionate person whose central purpose was to serve God, he used his unusual gift to assist troubled people for more than forty years. Putting himself into a sleeplike trance, he could answer questions with wisdom and precision—questions from those who suffered physically and had almost given up hope, questions from those who longed to understand themselves and find their way in life.

His discourses and answers given from this altered state of consciousness were stenographically logged and came to be called *readings*. Some 14,145 of them were recorded between 1901 and 1944. Upon his death in 1945, Cayce probably little realized the roles he had played: pioneer of the holistic health field, reinterpreter of metaphysical laws for our twentieth-century Judeo-Christian culture, forerunner of transpersonal psychology and the consciousness movement.

Edgar Cayce is a distinctly American phenomenon. Certainly he had a universal perspective, honoring deeply all the great religious traditions. And he was something of an internationalist in his concern for people worldwide. Yet the flavor of his biography and even the tone of his philosophy and psychology were unmistakably rooted in twentieth-century America. This fact is very important to many people

1

who have taken up his ideas and worked with them. Admittedly, the aim of spirituality in our country has been enhanced by teachings originating from Europe and the East. But many people resonate most clearly to a homegrown product. The Cayce readings offer an esoteric system that combines far-reaching concepts about spiritual realities with down-to-earth pragmatism.

The extraordinary teachings in Cayce's material are noteworthy for their *practicality* and *balance*. Rather than get us lost in abstract speculation, they bring us back to the here and now. Life itself, they affirm, is our opportunity to fulfill our potential—physically, mentally, and spiritually. No need to run off to a monastery on the other side of the world. No need to push oneself out of the body and into higher dimensions in order to find God. The Spirit is alive in the midst of daily living, if only we'll recognize it. That's practical spirituality, and it's fundamental to the many ideas that came through this unusual man.

Balance is just as important a principle, especially the balance between self-help psychology and the intervention of divine grace. The Cayce readings, like the precepts of the Buddha and psychiatrist Carl Jung, show a deep appreciation for the middle way, the equilibrium point between extremes. Individual growth and development may be realized through a harmonious interplay of personal effort on the one hand and surrender to a higher power on the other.

In essence, the Cayce philosophy paradoxically promises two things. First, you can create your future: You are an extraordinary being with powers to shape your life. Second, your future can create you: Your life has a destiny that draws you toward it. Each one of us, in other words, has the opportunity to be a cocreator with God.

This book is a guide to cocreativity. In specific ways it teaches us how to use two dozen "open secrets" that reveal the mysteries of living. It may sound like a contradiction to describe a secret as open and available, but the twenty-four spiritual principles that form the chapters of this handbook are secrets only in the sense that they are keys to unlock the doors of understanding. They are evident to anyone who is willing and able to look closely at life, who can honestly and objectively recognize that the Spirit is right here in our midst, not vacationing in some faraway heaven. For many centuries these concepts were deliberately shrouded in ritual and mysticism, relegated to so-called esotericism. But times change. Now millions of sincere seekers are ready to make practical use of this ancient knowledge.

Even though these twenty-four principles embody deep, important ideas, we don't have to become somber and overly serious in order to work with them. Thus this "handbook," while pragmatic, is also informal and even fun to use. Each of the brief chapters is filled with true stories from people's lives—inspiring, informative anecdotes that show how these ideas can really work on a practical, day-to-day basis.

The approach throughout this book is comparative: examples and illustrations are drawn from many sources, including the Bible, Jungian psychology, mythology, and current events. The point is to show how the Cayce material fits into and complements diverse systems of thought. Any teaching that is universal in its wisdom should lend itself to such parallels.

A handbook may also be used as a convenient reference volume. No doubt, as you read through this book for the first time, some of the chapters will touch you right where you live, addressing problems you currently face; others may seem interesting or intriguing but not as relevant to your challenges at the present time. As the months go by, however, you're likely to find yourself drawn to different chapters, suddenly more relevant because of a change in your situation.

The ideas in this book can and will work for you, depending on your willingness to try them out. Edgar Cayce founded an organization which he named the Association for Research and Enlightenment—because he believed that we learn and develop through a process of application and testing, and each of his twenty-four open secrets lends itself to this sort of personal, informal research. To augment the twenty-four concepts and deepen your ability to work with them, a brief exercise is described at the conclusion of every chapter. Give them a try!

This book contains the essence of the spiritual philosophy and psychology of the Cayce readings. Although it doesn't deal directly with Cayce's holistic concepts of health care, it does focus on the mental and spiritual factors that make physical health possible. You'll find only infrequent mention of the many fascinating topics that have made Cayce's name famous:

Atlantis, earth changes, ESP, past lives, and so on. Ancient civilizations, prophecies of change, astounding psychic feats, the mysteries of reincarnation . . . these are not at the heart of Cayce's material. If someone asks, "What's the Cayce legacy really all about?" the answer is cocreativity—responsibly shaping one's future with help from higher forces.

Take responsibility for your current situation, learn the universal principles that govern the game of life, and then make your life into a work of art: if you follow this three-step process as you apply the two dozen key ideas presented in this book, you'll become a more creative, productive, joyful citizen of this world. What better future could anyone hope to cocreate with God?

Basic Principles for Creating Your Future

PART ONE

Basic Principles for
Creating Your Future

Mind Is the Builder: What You Think, You Become

While in college Jerry attended a weekend seminar called "Preparing for the Future." Included in the seminar was a workshop that involved writing down in as much detail as possible just what you would like to be doing in twenty years. Jerry gave this exercise serious attention and did his best to visualize an ideal day twenty years into the future.

Participants concluded the exercise by putting the document into a sealed envelope, which would then be stashed away where it wouldn't be thought about or lost. All this Jerry did, and, as was expected, he forgot all about it. By a curious coincidence he found that envelope almost to the day twenty years later. As he read over the "ancient" document, he was amazed and tickled to discover that he was now actually living his projected scenario with uncanny accuracy.

What does this true story tell us—that Jerry was psychic and had successfully predicted the future? Maybe. But, more likely, what happened to Jerry is an illustration of something deeper and more profound, a principle that was articulated over and over in the psychic readings of Edgar Cayce: Mind is the builder. In other words, with the awesome power of your mind you can create your future, your situation in the world, even the very person you are. That power is a very special gift of the Creative Force, or God.

What is this gift of the mind, this fundamental aspect of your soul? Is it your ability to analyze and calculate? Is it your ability to visualize and imagine possibilities? Is it the mysterious part of you that concocts dreams every night while you sleep? Actually, it's all these things. Your mind is versatile and multifaceted, *and* it's the bridge between the realm of spirit and the world of physical reality.

The phrase *Mind is the builder* is usually found in the Cayce readings as part of a spiritual law that summarizes the creative process itself. In its entirety, the formula states, "Spirit is the life, mind is the builder, and the physical is the result." These simple words describe the most basic process of life. Understanding the concept gives you a potent tool in your pursuit of happiness.

The formula begins with the source and essence of all life, the spirit—the foundation of all things—the raw power from which everything is born. The Greeks named it *pneuma*. The Hindus call it *shakti;* the Sioux Indians, *wakonda*. In Western religions it is often referred to as the power of God. The Cayce readings label it the Creative Force, but regardless of its name, the spirit is the source of all that is.

How does this spiritual force express itself in the three-dimensional world of time, space, and form? Through the activity of mind. It's probably easier to grasp this formula with an analogy. Think of a slide projector. The light bulb corresponds to the source of life, the screen to the material world. The *slide* represents the mind! That transparent film takes the source light, shapes it into pattern and color, and projects the image onto the material screen.

The mind works in the same way. With a unique mixture of attitudes, emotions, logical analysis, and intuition, it first creates a pattern. Using the pure energy of spirit, the mind shapes a "thought-form," which is analogous to a single slide. Of course, you have created *many* different thought-forms, all stored as memory patterns, like the slides in a carousel tray. At any moment of the day one of your slides is chosen from the memory storehouse, is reanimated by the source light, and eventually projects into your three-dimensional world of physical matter. These thought-forms are quite real; although they aren't a "physical" reality, they *shape* the physical world according to their patterns. One Cayce reading says simply that thoughts are things and are as real as a pin stuck into your hand.

At first it may take a little effort to appreciate the reality of this thought-form world. Where is a thought? What does it look like? How can it be real if you can't grasp or measure it? Both Cayce and the Swiss psychiatrist Carl Jung describe the world of thought as the "fourth dimension," the dimension of ideas. For example, what makes this book you are reading real? Is it the weight of the paper and the color of the ink? That's a superficial explanation. A more profound answer to this question suggests that the "reality" of thought may be embodied in the *ideas* that come to life in your mind through the miracle of the written word. Even more fascinating, the same idea can be shared with any number of other people scattered throughout the world and even throughout the generations. An idea isn't limited to space *or* time.

Dreams often give us a peek into the creative realm of thought-forms. Consider the following story. A woman came to Edgar Cayce and asked for a reading to interpret a strange dream she had had. She had dreamed that she was holding her arms out before her with the palms turned upward. Encircling both forearms was a series of diamond bracelets. It so happened that she and her husband had been trying to conceive a child for several months. The interpretation was that on the night of the dream they had succeeded in their effort. The bracelets in the dream symbolized the joy that the woman would feel cradling the baby in her arms. This much of the story by itself is enough to make one marvel at the subtle faculties of the mind. But even more remarkable is that the woman's sister, living miles away, had had the same dream the same night! She, too, had dreamed of her sister, her forearms bedecked with diamond bracelets—an illustration of how, through the unlimited nature of the fourth-dimensional world, we can be made sensitive to the thought-forms of others.

How Long Does It Take for a Thought to Build into the Physical?

If spirit is the life, mind is the builder, and the physical is the result, *how long* does it take for the mind to project a fourth-dimensional thought-form into the world of concrete physical reality?

That's a good question. Unfortunately, there isn't a simple answer. The timing depends on many factors. For example, before a house can exist, it must be built, but before it can be built with wood or stone, it needs to be designed. That design starts with an *idea* in the mind of an architect.

Then, once the fourth-dimensional thought-form image has been created, how long does it take for the design to be translated into a physical house? First, how grand or complicated is the design? If it's a log cabin, it may be built in a few days; if it's a castle, it will take longer. Second, how much sweat and elbow grease will be applied to the project? If the builder works ten hours a day, the house will materialize twice as fast as it will if the builder works only five hours a day. In essence, the time gap between "mind is the builder" and "the physical is the result" boils down to two factors: the scope of what's being built and the perseverance of those who are laboring for it.

For most people the lack of consistent, persistent effort is the obstacle. Most of us are good at dreaming up grand ideas, but we fail to work at them until they can move from the fourth dimension to the third. For example, a high school student was lying on the living room couch, lamenting to his mother that he had only a few days to complete a term paper. Of course, upon being questioned, he admitted that the assignment had been given several weeks earlier. Then, in the midst of a stretch, he yawned and said, "I guess I was just made to be a procrastinator, and there's not a thing I can do about it."

When people with a tendency toward procrastination asked Cayce how to succeed with their projects, he usually gave the same terse advice: "Work like thunder!"

The Hatching Process

The spirit is the life, mind is the builder, the physical is the result—this formula explains the creative process. But if we examine it more carefully, what clues emerge to tell us more about how these steps unfold?

First comes *conception*, also known as inspiration, the awakening of a possibility of something new. Second is *incubation*, a time of accumulating energies. Think of the idea as an embryo or an egg that needs nourishment and time; through incubation, it accrues the energy needed to penetrate the world of matter. Finally, when the moment is right, the inspiration starts to materialize. That's birth or, better yet, the *hatching* of the idea.

Many mythologies throughout the world—Greek, Finnish, Hindu, Japanese, and Egyptian, to name a few—use the image of the egg to describe the creation of the universe. In one version of an Egyptian myth, the first act of creation began with the formation of an egg out of the primeval water. From this egg broke forth Ra, the sun god and the immediate cause of all life on earth. The egg motif is still with us today when we speak of hatching a plot or hatching an idea.

The world is full of "overnight successes" who in fact spent years honing their craft or deepening their study. One young writer, named Barry Kemp, suddenly moved to Hollywood and seemed to take the town by storm. First he worked as a staff comedy writer for the hit series *Taxi;* then he went on to create the blockbuster hit comedies *Coach* and *Newhart*. To a casual observer he was the classic overnight success—yet for years Barry had crawled out of bed every morning at five o'clock to spend two hours writing television scripts that no one ever read!

That's the incubation period that precedes the hatching. It's a period not of idleness but of inner work, of preparation for the opportunities that *will* come as a direct consequence of mental building.

The Mental Body

It's important to remember that the mind is building with every thought. A current slogan reminds us that "you are what you eat," and in a very real sense that's true. If you eat an apple, your digestive system breaks it down into elemental parts, your blood carries the elements throughout your body, and your cells assimilate it. All this happens in a marvelously coordinated effort.

Just as the food you eat is assimilated into your physical body, so is every thought you think assimilated into what the Cayce readings call your "mental body." This mental body is the living memory of all the thoughts, attitudes, and actions that you choose—moment to moment—throughout your life. Does the notion of a mental "body" seem strange to you? Well, consider this: Cayce maintained that the mental body becomes your home when you are finished with your current physical incarnation! In other words, after death you live in the body that you have mentally built during your life.

This concept isn't limited to the Cayce readings. In *A Christmas Carol*, the famous yuletide story by Charles Dickens, the disagreeable protagonist Ebenezer Scrooge meets the spirit of his deceased cohort in usury, Jacob Marley. Marley's spirit visits him dragging a huge chain. When Scrooge asks where he got it, Marley shrieks, "I made this chain link by link and yard by yard!"

Of course, a positive view may just as well be taken in regard to this maxim. Each of us has the power to build a *paradise* through our thoughts, attitudes, and actions.

The Near Death Experience

Most people are now familiar with the term *near death experience*. There are thousands of individuals who, for one reason or another, have technically "died" yet with modern medical technology have been successfully revived. Researchers have interviewed many who have had this experience, and it's striking to see the common themes and images which thread together these different accounts. People report viewing their physical bodies from above, dispassionate observers of what's going on in the hospital room, for example. Then they turn and move into another space or realm, a process which they often describe as passing through a tunnel. At the end there is usually an encounter with a being of love and light. Sometimes this being simply tells the person that he or she must go back. However, on other occasions this being asks, "What have you done with your life?" When such a question is raised, individuals in the near death experience are presented with a panorama of their entire life—every action, every thought, even the influence of those actions and thoughts on others. Often they describe this panorama as being three-dimensional, in full color, with every scene appearing simultaneously. There is probably no better description of what it would be like to live in one's mental body.

There Are Thoughts and There Are Thoughts

What is the natural reaction to giving serious consideration to the principle that mind is the builder? Anxiety, probably— nervous concern that some of your attitudes and emotions aren't ones you'd like to carry with you into eternity.

Anna carried this anxiety to an extreme. She speculated that a single, truly bad thought could ruin beyond repair her bliss in the afterlife. Her concern grew until she developed a nearly obsessive fear of thinking. Then, one day, she was fortunate enough to share this concern with a wise old woman who had spent years living the philosophy found in the Cayce readings. This elderly woman put her troubled mind to rest.

"Your mind is like a tree, and the thoughts that enter your mind are like birds," she said. "It's not so important which birds light on a branch of your tree for a moment and then fly on. What matters is which birds you allow to build a *nest* in your tree and make a home there."

There's probably not a fleeting thought that we all haven't held at one time or another, but the thoughts that build our reality are those we feed on day after day.

Overriding the Automatic Pilot

Our minds are building reality with every moment, but most of the time we aren't conscious of this creative process. Our attitudes and thought patterns become habitual. We don't see how frequently we keep building and rebuilding some old favorites. Of course, some of these mental habits may be desirable, but others might benefit from a change if we could only recognize them clearly.

There are a couple of ways you can begin to wake up to your habits of thinking. The first approach is dream study. Since dreams occur when you're asleep, it may sound paradoxical to state that they can help you become aware of your mental habits. But dreams are an adventure into the world of thought-forms. In them you confront directly some of the patterns you've been sustaining with your attitudes and emotions. Dreams help you recognize more clearly what you are doing each day at a fourth-dimensional level. With practice plus some basic instruction with interpretational skills, you can discover more and more about your inner world.

The best way to enhance your dream recall is to sincerely want to work with your dreams. Strong intention and desire are powerful agents. Then follow a few simple techniques. Put a pad of paper or dream journal on a bedside table. As you're falling asleep, repeat silently to yourself several times, "I will remember my dreams when I wake up." When you do wake up, spend a moment lying still in bed. Allow those elusive dream images to come back to mind. Most likely what you'll remember is the conclusion of a dream, so try to remember the sequence of action in reverse by asking yourself, "What was I doing just before that?" Then be sure to write down your dream as soon as you can. If you wait until later in the day, you may find that many of the details are lost.

Another approach, "self-observation," enables you to observe your own thinking process *in the moment*. The Cayce readings called this "standing aside and watching yourself go by." Through self-observation you can begin to see which attitudes constantly run through your mind as an inner dialogue or talk. You may start to recognize which circumstances set off particular emotional responses. In fact, the presence of powerful emotions *intensifies* the building process. For example, love and hate both provide extra energy for the creative mind. Of course, the question is, Which emotions do you want to use in building your mental body?

With self-observation you can also begin to recognize the different "roles" you play and the accompanying phrases you use in speaking to yourself throughout the day. Sometimes self-observation is a humbling experience, but it can also be fun. It's always enlightening. You may discover that you've been feeding your mind phrases such as "I can't do that" or "I'm so stupid" or "I just hate that!" This may not be a happy revelation, but at the same time you can make a conscious effort to feed your mind *new* phrases such as "Nothing ventured, nothing gained" or "I'm making real progress" or "I'm going to learn a lot from this no matter what happens." The new affirmations may feel artificial at first because you aren't used to them, but they are the first stage in a valuable reorientation of your mind. Small as these efforts may seem, they put you on the road to a more constructive, successful future. Remember this saying from Lao-tzu's *Tao Tê Ching* (Chapter 64), a kernel of Chinese Taoist wisdom: "The journey of a thousand miles begins with a single step." The long journey really comes down to this key: You are a creative, spiritual being, and what you do with your mind determines your destiny.

EXERCISE

One way to see more clearly what you are building mentally is through the practice of self-observation, what the Cayce readings called "standing aside and watching yourself go by." The focus of your observations will be the inner world of your thoughts and feelings rather than events in the outer world. It's not easy to sustain attention for this kind of self-observation, but try to do it three times a day, even if it's for just a minute at a time.

What you'll probably recognize is your own inner talk, a mental dialogue that goes on among aspects of yourself. What's the quality of your inner talk? Argumentative? Optimistic? Self-condemning? Hopeful? Recognize the kind of future you are creating with those thoughts and feelings.

PRINCIPLE #2

Changing Anything Starts with Motives and Ideals

Take a moment to imagine the kind of future you hope to have. Be specific. What types of people do you want in your life? How will you be spending your time? Where will you live and work? You may even wish to write down this image of what you see in store for you.

Now, in order to turn that dream into a reality, some changes are necessary. Outer conditions may need to be modified, but you'll be required to alter some of your own thoughts and feelings as well.

Exactly *how* does one go about making changes in one's life? Dozens of books and courses are available, each promising some secret method to help make your life different: weight loss programs, stop-smoking classes, and subliminal tapes, to name a few. However, success does not lie in a gimmick or with any particular technique. Change begins with your values, motives, and ideals.

In 1942 Margaret, a forty-year-old woman who was working as a clerk, wrote to Edgar Cayce and asked for a reading, the thirteenth she had received from him. Her series of readings had begun ten years earlier with information on her anemia, but she also suffered from anxiety and depression. Through the years she had struggled to improve her physical and emotional health, yet she had had a great deal of trouble effectively taking charge of her life. Now she again asked for advice regarding her health, home life, work, and general welfare.

Reminding her that "mind is the builder," the reading told her that she needed to build on spiritual ideals if she wanted a more positive future. Her mind could just as easily destroy her if it built on selfish desires and interests. To emphasize the necessity of having a spiritual ideal, Cayce boldly affirmed that the most important experience of any individual in any lifetime is to establish a spiritual ideal.

The message couldn't be stated any more plainly, and it's directed to every single one of us. Before anything can change for the better—before your mind can truly create a brighter future—you need to establish the right purposes.

Let's expand on the metaphor that likens the mind to a carpenter who creates new buildings. Who is the architect in this analogy? Who draws the blueprints and establishes a pattern for the mind to follow in its creativity? The answer: your motives, ideals, and values.

What are your personal values? What do you hold as an ideal? Many individuals have difficulty even understanding these questions. Why? Because most people let *unconscious* motives and values drive their thinking and feeling. These ideals lie hidden like the gears of a clock that mysteriously make the hands turn. For most of us, beliefs and values are so embedded in the cultural atmosphere that we don't even recognize or see them—it's like trying to observe the air we breathe.

The Fifth Dimension

Both Cayce and Jung described the mental realm, the realm of ideas, as a "fourth dimension"—a domain extending beyond the limits of time and space. The three-dimensional reality of material life is a depiction of the four-dimensional thought-form world. However, if ideas give rise to physical things, what's the source of these fourth-dimensional ideas? It makes sense to imagine a fifth dimension that would be the origin of any thought. Such a level of reality in the invisible realms of the soul is where values and motives live. Any attitude or thought becomes an expression of *some* ideal, conscious or unconscious. There are no value-free ideas because every idea has an implicit ideal behind it.

Although ideals reside in a higher dimension than thought, they may not necessarily be attuned to the spirit of the Creator; for example, selfish motives give rise to selfish thoughts. Also, many of our values are products of our families and society, and sometimes these sources are not very spiritually enlightened. For years psychologists and philosophers have attempted to map this remote terrain of the fifth dimension. From his psychoanalytic work with patients, Sigmund Freud concluded that all our values are ultimately rooted in primitive biological drives. Carl Jung, by contrast, asserted that while physical desires shape many of our values, there is nevertheless a spiritual element that can raise us above mere carnal concerns. The noted mythologist Joseph Campbell grouped human motives into four categories: the drive to eat, the drive to procreate, the impulse to conquer, and, finally, compassion. The first two are clearly animal drives, while the third is distinctly human and the fourth constitutes an awakening of spiritual awareness.

The philosophy of the Cayce readings takes a bold stand. Although allowing for carnal, or "earth-earthy," desires, the readings insist that our *true* nature is spiritual and that our original values or ideals are the same as God's. These are the same ideals that have been exemplified by the great spiritual teachers throughout history: love, patience, forgiveness, kindness, and compassion.

Ideals versus Ideas

Ideals are not the same as *ideas*, although it's easy to confuse them. Religion can be a rich source of spiritual ideals, but when zealots force their religion onto others with a "You must believe" attitude, they confuse their religion's ideals with human ideas. One way of understanding the difference between the two is to think of ideas—thoughts, for example—as things. This notion is useful because you can own material things, and your ideas are a kind of possession. When you persuade others to accept them, you increase the value of your ideas. The more people you persuade to agree with your ideas, the more power and security you derive from them. Therefore, "Convert or die" has been the battle cry of every religious war in history as well as the motto of every religious zealot.

Ideals, by contrast, are not possessions. You can't *own* an ideal—quite the contrary. For an ideal to become effective in your life, you must allow it to own *you*. For example, you can have very strong ideas about Jesus and work hard to push them onto others, but until you allow forgiveness and tolerance to influence your thoughts, feelings, and actions directly, you have not accepted this ideal. By *giving yourself* to an ideal or value, you allow it to change you.

What's Your Motive?

Two men were approached and asked to contribute to a worthwhile building project that was intended to provide shelter for the homeless. One man was wealthy and gave $1,000. He had been looking for a tax write-off, and when he learned that his name would be listed in the paper as a major donor, he was quick to contribute. The other man was of modest means, but he gave what he could—which was much less than $1,000—because he had seen the suffering of the homeless and empathized with their pain. These two men had the same idea: to give money. They performed identical acts of service. However, their motives were entirely different.

No doubt, ideas and acts of kindness are important to building a happy future, but the motivations that spur those actions are just as important. The mind creates with the stuff of values and motives. Our ideals are the very substance, the building materials, with which our attitudes and emotions construct our future. By analogy, architectural plans designate not only the shape and size of a new structure but whether it is to be made of solid concrete or unstable clay. We can build an inner life based on greed or self-interest, or we can build with compassion and empathy. *Why* we do something is just as important as *what* we do.

Conversely, people can share the same ideal and yet have quite different ideas about how to manifest it. Republicans and Democrats alike want peace and prosperity for the nation, but any political debate will demonstrate that they have very different ideas about how to achieve those goals. In the same way, we can have strong disagreements with someone about how to manifest some value and yet remain united in our love for it. Cayce was surrounded by a team of bright, strong-willed followers. Quite often each member of that group had a different *idea* about how some task should be accomplished. Readings given to these supporters often reminded them that it was all right to have a variety of *ideas* as long as they shared a common *ideal*.

How to Connect with Your Spiritual Ideal for Positive Change

Already at the center of your being lives a spiritual ideal, whether you have ever been conscious of it or not. Even though this core ideal is the same for everyone, defining it is a very personal matter. That ideal is a state of consciousness that resonates to the very nature of God. Since each of us is a spark of the Creator, we share in that divine impulse or motive. We can't totally define this spiritual ideal; no word or phrase can articulate it completely. But we can choose personally meaningful words that identify our own particular version of it. Then, as we keep this ideal clearly in mind, it helps us build positive change in all areas of our lives.

At least two useful methods can help you decide on a word or phrase that describes this highest spiritual value. One is to think of people whom you deeply respect or revere. Major religious figures are certainly candidates, but other, less famous role models may serve just as well. Ask yourself what it is in them that awakens your admiration. What are their values and character traits that make them so special to you? The qualities you list may be ones you'll want to include in the wording for your spiritual ideal.

Another way of finding words to describe your ideal is to think back to moments in your own history when you felt "lifted up" in some way. Your peak moments in life provide clues about your core spiritual ideal. Sometimes these extraordinary events may come during prayer, meditation, or dream experiences that give you a glimpse of a higher reality. Perhaps one inspiration occurred when you were out in nature or during a moment of special tenderness. Maybe a peak experience happened when you acted with loving selflessness.

As you resurrect those special moments from your past, feel their impact on you. Then let those feelings crystallize into a word or phrase that best captures this inner experience. The words you write down will describe your best understanding of the spiritual ideal.

Setting Mental and Physical Ideals

The personal wording you choose for the universal spiritual ideal is a kind of symbol. And, like any symbol, it means more than you can grasp consciously; it manifests just a small part of itself while reaching into the deeper levels of your mind, the way an iceberg submerged into the ocean reveals only its tip. But it's the hidden part that has the power to shape your thoughts and actions.

How can you tell if the symbolic words you've chosen for your spiritual ideal really correspond to the essential core of your soul, what Cayce called your individuality? Confirmation comes from the attitudes, emotions, and actions it draws out of you. These thoughts, feelings, and behaviors are your mental and physical ideals.

The following story illustrates the process. A boy going to high school in the mid-1960s found a symbol for his spiritual ideal in the guise of the contemporary folk trio Peter, Paul, and Mary. His first experience with this symbol was purely at a feeling level. All he knew was that their music held a strange and powerful magnetism for him; it stirred things within him he couldn't express but could only feel deeply.

Later, he heard words and phrases in their songs that helped him articulate more clearly the powerful impact this group had on him. He heard lyrics about justice, ringing in the bells of freedom, and loving one another as if we were all brothers and sisters. The words *harmonious, loving justice* became another way for him to describe symbolically the core values within his own soul.

The words combined with the deep feeling inspired by the music and began to shape the boy's ethics. He grew to appreciate the values of fairness, equality, compassion, hope, and courage. These attitudes and emotions became his *mental ideals*, specific ways in which his spiritual ideal came to life in his mental world.

In turn, these values helped shape his activities. On a practical level, they inspired him to study the artistic disciplines of guitar and musical harmony. In a larger perspective, they guided him in his choice of reading material, in his selection of friends, and in dozens of other daily decisions.

Those ideals continued to direct him throughout his adult years. When his actions began authentically to reflect his mental ideals, they became *physical ideals*. Even when he couldn't manifest his ideals perfectly, he would try to act in ways that at least approached them, by speaking fairly, looking for the common humanity in each person, and telling the truth as he understood it. Most of all, he strove to generate harmony and equality in all his relationships. The application of his physical ideals never made him rich, and he never became a famous folk singer. Nevertheless, he found strength in feeling that he was a part of the same great work that had inspired the three singers who first symbolized his spiritual ideal.

Putting Ideals to the Test

What happens when a person tries to change his or her personal patterns by applying new motives and ideals? Eighty-five people familiar with the Cayce readings attempted to do just that during a three-week research project. As volunteers, they agreed to follow certain steps at home. The experiment was designed to test, over time, the effectiveness of thinking consciously about and recommitting to values and ideals.

All eighty-five people completed workbook exercises to identify problem areas in their lives. Difficult relationships and addictive behaviors were the most frequent examples. Then each participant shortened the list to one core problem, arrived at on the basis of a strong *desire* to make a change happen in that situation and a feeling that the time was right—that the circumstance was *ripe for change*.

In the days that followed each individual gave careful consideration to the values, motives, and ideals that seemed to apply to his or her special problem area. Journal-writing exercises provided a way to make clear statements of intention. Through conscious application the ideals became a living reality rather than well-intentioned fantasies.

At the end of three weeks the participants provided a written report on their experiences. How successful had they been in achieving the changes they desired? Some had attained their goal, but others found that the problems were deep-seated and would probably require months of effort before positive results could be achieved.

However, one of the most interesting findings was measured by a multiple-choice questionnaire completed just prior to and after the three-week experimental period. Developed by psychologist J. B. Rotter, the questionnaire evaluates the so-called locus of control, that is, the extent to which a person believes that the forces that shape and control his or her life are either external or internal. Over the three weeks the group demonstrated a highly significant change on the test scores. Their feelings and perceptions had shifted to reflect a growing awareness that such life-shaping forces reside *within oneself*.

The Cayce readings indicate that working with values, motives, and ideals is fundamental to personal growth. In fact, it's considered the most effective entry point in the sequence of steps that leads to change. However, there are no shortcuts to creating a positive future. Paying careful attention to ideals puts you in touch with an invaluable resource: the power that resides in your soul to take charge of your life.

EXERCISE

The focus of this exercise is on setting reachable, short-term behavior goals (physical ideals) for shaping a positive future. But first spend some time deciding on your personal expression of a spiritual ideal. That means a central value that gives your life meaning.

Then pick one area of your life that you want to change for the better. Decide on some mental ideals (i.e., optimal thoughts and feelings) and physical ideals (i.e., positive activities) that can apply. For example, that area might be your diet, a relationship, or your career situation. As you make a short list of physical ideals related to one particular part of your life, use these hints:

1. A mental ideal may suggest a good physical ideal. For example, in your career, an ideal attitude of enthusiasm might suggest an ideal behavior of showing up thirty minutes early.

2. Choose behavior goals that are *reachable*. In other words, give yourself room to be successful during the coming week. Later, you'll want to commit to more challenging physical ideals in that particular life circumstance, but start out first with small steps that are attainable.

God Is Living—
Active and Responsive

"God is dead!" or so Friedrich Nietzsche announced in the late nineteenth century. In the 1930s Nietzsche's claim inspired a whole movement led by writers, artists, and philosophers who called themselves existentialists. According to these followers, we have no help beyond our own individual effort. God—if there ever was such a deity—long ago departed or died.

But doesn't something in your soul react to this sort of cynicism? If you look carefully at your life, you'll see evidence for the opposite point of view: God is alive. And that's much more complex than simply admitting that God *exists*. Rocks *exist*—so do the stars. Both may even be alive in some way, but they also seem distant, cold, and uninvolved with us.

The world is full of people who believe in God, yet their concept leaves no room for intimacy and a direct relationship with a living force. For example, some people imagine God to be an all-powerful and changeless force for right and good. Others suppose God to be a remote parent with certain unbendable expectations.

Perhaps you catch yourself occasionally believing in this sort of God—awesome but missing some of the components usually associated with truly being alive. Think for a moment about such qualities, characterized by adjectives like *creative*, *vital*, *dynamic*, *active*, and *responsive*. Aren't those the kinds of words you might use to describe *yourself* on days when you're feeling full of life? Wouldn't the same descriptions fit a living God?

God Is Responsive to You and Active in Your Life

These two features were especially important in the way the Cayce readings described God: *responsive* to individual needs and *active* in human affairs. You can have interactions with these divine forces and directly encounter the sacred in your own life. As Cayce told one man who dreamed of the deity as a businessman: This is a God who is alive in daily affairs, someone you "can do business with."

To better understand the mysteries of life, recognize that a living God is aware of and concerned about your needs and difficulties. Jesus said as much when He promised that "even the hairs of your head are all counted" (Luke 12:7) and that God "calleth his own sheep by name and leads them out." (John 10:3)

But this vital, dynamic God is never satisfied simply to be sympathetic. The Creative Forces take *initiatives,* reaching out to all of humanity as well as to individuals like you. On a *regular basis* events and situations arise that can be understood as divine initiatives in your life. As Dr. Harmon Bro put it, "God is loose in the world, stirring up loving mischief."

So what kind of image of God might you create? Not a superhuman being, certainly, but still a creative force with which you can have a personal relationship. God is not a person yet is very personal. The Creator is a friend and constant companion, a source of guidance, support, and encouragement through all the changing currents of life.

An intimate relationship is perhaps exactly what the Creative Forces desire for you. How can you begin to cultivate such a dynamic and spirited alliance with God? The first step is to believe that it's possible.

How Can You Prove God?

Where's the proof? Where's the evidence that a living God stands ready to be active and responsive? It's a fair question, and the answer may come from two sources.

First are experiences that come as gifts. At times you may have caught a glimpse of some confirmation, without necessarily looking for or expecting anything. These situations tend to happen in the midst of great difficulties. For example, in a period of deep discouragement you might have unexpectedly felt, even for just a moment, that life is good and purposeful.

A second source of evidence may come from your own willingness "to give God a try." In other words, a medicine cannot be proved effective unless and until it's swallowed, and then it's proved only if and when it improves your health. In the same way God can be made manifest through an initial step of faith—by your acting "as if" God were with you, sharing your joys and sorrows, lending support and guidance.

Cayce's readings often assigned skeptical people a task: to act as if some proposition were true, to give an idea a chance by temporarily assuming its validity and watching for results. Propositions based on truth will hold up to this kind of test; they'll yield surprising results. In light of this you might try assuming that God is in fact alive—active and responsive— and then live your life for some time guided by that point of view. Many people like you have eventually found proof enough of the truth in this way.

Of course, no one can prove or disprove God empirically. No argument or laboratory test can unequivocally nail down the answer to this ultimate question. But just as you experience your own consciousness—your own sense of "being"—you can personally encounter the reality and abiding presence of the Creative Force. You merely have to be willing to take the first step.

This process is described in a folk song that was popularized by the Kingston Trio. The song is about a dusty well, a bottle of water, and a note by a mysterious "Desert Pete." In the song, a man lost in the desert without water stumbles onto an old water pump. He tries the pump, but it produces no water. Discouraged, he sits down under a tree, and much to his surprise, he finds a bottle of water and an attached note. The note is from Desert Pete, and says that the bottle of water is for priming the pump. All one has to do is pour it down the well like crazy, and you'll get all the water you can drink. Well, of course, the man is torn. He wants desperately to drink the water he has in hand rather than pour it down a pump that may be as dry as a bone, but he finally chooses to take the step of faith. Of course, he succeeds in finding water, drinks his fill, and leaves the bottle full for the next traveler.

Like the person in the song, we are often thirsty. We may

be doubtful about the existence of a bountiful source of relief, but we can find out only by giving something first. What we have to give is the benefit of the doubt. We have to say, "I'm going to believe that God is aware of me and cares about me. And I'm going to let that belief influence my attitudes and actions. I'm going to 'try out' God."

What Does God Promise?

As you "try out" God, however, it's important to guard against the very human tendency to say, "God, give me this and *then* I'll believe in you." During war, don't some people pray for God to help defeat the enemy? Don't some people pray to be delivered from drought, or flood, or bank failures? And when we suffer from life's whammies, how do we reconcile our failed prayers with the belief in a loving and responsive God?

Mythologist Joseph Campbell points out that no authentic religions promise us deliverance from suffering. They will instruct us on how to suffer *purposefully;* they'll show us how to find strength and spiritual support in our suffering; they'll promise us inner peace in the midst of suffering—but they won't promise us an escape. Suffering is a part of life. If we ask the Creator to prove its own existence by protecting us from suffering, we are misunderstanding the nature of life and the creative power that lies within test and trial.

A fair question, then, is, What good is God? Why should I be concerned about God one way or another?

If it's true that God, or the Creative Force, is the source and essence of all life, then God is also the essence and source of your life and mine. God is life itself. In other words, God isn't like the chairman of the board or the president of the company, who may not even know you exist. Rather, God is like the blood flowing in your veins or the air that you breathe or the orchestrator of your dreams at night. The Creative Force is immanent; it is present in all your experiences. As the psalmist says, "If I take the wings of the morning, and settle at the farthest limits of the sea, even there your hand shall lead me" (Psalms 139:9–10). Or as Jesus says, "Yet not one of them will fall to the ground apart from your Father" (Matthew 10:29).

How Does God Relate to You?

God not only is aware of and concerned about you but also is active and working in your life. Jesus tells the parable of the lost sheep in Matthew 18:12. If a shepherd has one hundred sheep and one gets lost, the shepherd will leave the ninety-nine and go in search of the one that is lost. God, or the Universal Consciousness or the Creative Force, initiates relationships with us. If we learn to watch and observe carefully, we can see evidence of this in our own experience.

Have you ever wrestled with a particular issue in life only to find yourself "accidentally" meeting someone who not only understands your situation or concern but actually has advice or information that is just what you need at the moment? Perhaps you've had a dream about a friend or relative in which the person seemed distressed or in need, and then later, when you called or visited that person, you discovered that you were really needed at that particular moment. Or maybe you just "stumble onto" a book or a magazine article that leads you to a whole new area of interest or activity.

Such experiences may be seen as God, or the universe, extending a helping hand through "coincidence," through encounters with people or ideas that seem accidental but have an impact on your life that is anything but trivial. You can think of these as examples of the grace of God or the gracefulness of a caring universe. Carl Jung used the term *synchronicity* to describe these meaningful coincidences.

None of this is intended to depict God as some master controller, sitting in a vast computer booth somewhere, arranging matches, throwing down thunderbolts, or otherwise meddling as He or She sees fit. Such an image reinforces a distant and rather threatening view of the God Force. Rather, this view is of a very personal God (not separate from you or me), a God who is very active in our lives but not arbitrary. We can turn to the East for help with this concept of a living God.

The Eastern religions see God in a nonanthropomorphic way, as the essential unity of all creation. The Creator is the living spirit behind every manifestation of the phenomenal world—not only the world of matter and energy but the world of time as well. The word for this all-pervasive essence is the *Tao*, meaning the "proper flow" or the "appropriate balance" of life. In other words, God is a force that seeks harmony and balance. If we, as free agents, create imbalances in our lives, the harmonizing flow of God will bring to us experiences that will help us regain our balance—not because some master controller looks down from a cloud and says, "Uh-oh, shame on you!" but because life, which is God, seeks balance and beauty and harmony.

But God is more than just compensatory. In other words, God is not just counterbalancing your actions. The Creative Force has a plan, a design, for every part of creation, including you. Because of this plan, life will bring to you just the experiences you need to fully manifest your potential. Eastern philosophy puts it this way: "When the student is ready, the teacher will appear." Now, the teacher may be a person or even a book or movie. More often than not it's a situation. God, or life, brings to you just what you need at the moment. In that way, every moment is an opportunity. The moment may bring an opportunity to correct an imbalance that you've created either consciously or unconsciously. Or it may bring you an opportunity to manifest further your potential and purpose. In either case, God is interacting with you in a very intentional way. God cares about you and is working with you personally at every single moment of your life.

God initiates relationships with you. God brings to you people, events, and experiences that will help you along the road of life.

The "Accidents" That Last

Here is the story of how a series of "accidents" threaded together wove for one man the greatest treasures of his life. The story begins at a time when he was very confused and unhappy about his life. One year after graduating from college with a theater degree and subsequently breaking up with his girlfriend, he was pining away in a small midwestern town, teaching seventh-grade English. He was living by himself in an upstairs apartment miles away from any of his friends and even farther away from the chance to live his dreams.

One day he took his seventh-grade class on a field trip to his old college and "just happened" to run into a former classmate, who shoved an address into his hand. "Write to this man," the friend said. "He's the head of the drama department at that university and is offering scholarships."

The young man acted on the lead and was awarded an audition. Then, shortly before the appointed date for the audition, for no known reason, he chose to go home for lunch rather than stay at school, which was his usual custom. Sitting on a chair, eating an orange, he heard the phone ring. He answered it and heard the pleasant voice of a young woman. She had called from the university to alert him that there was a change in the audition date. They had a very pleasant conversation, and for days afterward he found himself trying to visualize her face.

The audition came, he did well, and to his joy he was admitted to the program. For two years he studied with the best artists in the field. The woman whose voice he had heard on the phone turned out to be a student also. After graduation they were married, and in the following fifteen years the two of them built a life together that was nourished in part by their mutual experience in that theater program. Thus, what had seemed to be a series of coincidences proved to have profound consequences in his life.

Can you remember some event or encounter that seemed purely accidental yet in time proved to be pivotal in your life's journey? This might be seen as the hand of God operating within your sphere of life.

God not only calls you by name but opens doors, beckons you through them, and says, "Come with me. We have work to do."

EXERCISE

This is an exercise which is largely focused on expanding your perceptions—becoming aware of influences that usually go unnoticed.

Try to become more observant of your inner and outer worlds. Watch for indications of a living, caring God, one who takes the initiative.

You may experience this in a variety of ways, for example, in "accidental, coincidental" meetings with people who can help you. On other occasions you may observe these initiatives as small, subtle signs. Pay special attention also to your sleep experiences. A living, caring God may express guidance either directly or symbolically through a dream.

Then, as you recognize these initiatives from the spiritual world, try to be responsive and make practical use of them in the material world. What do they invite you to do? How are they showing you ways to be more sensitive, creative, or productive?

PRINCIPLE #4

All is One—
Everything Is Connected

"All is one." These words may conjure up images of a 1960s flower child draped with beads, gazing dreamily into space and spouting cosmic platitudes. The phrase *All is one*, along with the pictures it stirs up, seems completely irrelevant to the hard realities of day-to-day living. The modern world *appears* diverse and fragmented, anything but whole. So how can the concept of oneness be true?

This dilemma was on the mind of Edgar Cayce's friend and supporter Morton Blumenthal, an intelligent, curious, ambitious stockbroker who had made a fortune playing the stock market game. In the mid-1920s Morton and his brother, Edwin, became intrigued with Cayce's gift and eventually financed his lifelong dream of a hospital. Through the next several years Morton received 468 psychic readings from Cayce, more than any other single individual. With the help of those readings, he attempted to grasp the big picture of a universe operating according to spiritual laws. In March 1929, during such a reading on spiritual laws, Morton asked several questions about how to introduce these truths to newly interested people. From his trance state, Cayce answered emphatically that the first lesson *for six months* should be *one*—oneness of God, oneness of human relations, oneness of force, oneness of time, oneness of purpose, oneness in every effort.

This was a forceful admonition, and six months sounded like a long time. We might suspect that there's more to the subject of oneness than simply stating, "All is one!" and letting it go at that. Indeed, as we dig into the Cayce material, we find thread after golden thread that weave this vast universe into a single grand design.

Oneness of All Force

How can we get a better handle on this principle of oneness? First, we might look at its different *expressions*. For example, if we understand that there is only one force in the universe, then everything that exists—from stars to spiders—is a manifestation and expression of this one creative energy or life force.

In his popular science book *Cosmos*, Carl Sagan is photographed next to an oak tree. The caption reads, "Close relatives: an oak tree and a human." In other words, both trees and humans (in fact, all types of organic life) are essentially made of the same carbon, hydrogen, and oxygen atoms. And as nuclear physicists delve ever deeper into the realm of subatomic particles, it's becoming increasingly evident that the rich stew of the material universe is boiling up from a single mysterious ingredient. Indeed, it was Einstein who embarked on a lifelong quest to discover the single underlying formula that would represent the unification of the entire mechanism of the universe. Scientists are still building on his monumental effort.

However, the idea that there is one, fundamental force can be carried even further. Not only is the physical world rooted in one underlying energy, both the physical and mental worlds share a common essence. Remember that your mind—your attitudes, emotions, thoughts, and imagination—creates your reality. *Spirit is the life, mind is the builder, and the physical is the result*. This sequence traces the pattern of creative action and highlights the underlying unity of all creation.

As an example of this, consider how white light can be broken into the colors of the rainbow by a prism. A similar process happens in our own souls as the one fundamental force separates or refracts into attitudinal, emotional, and physical components. Red light isn't essentially different from blue. They're both light; they just vibrate at different frequencies. In the same way, thoughts or feelings are not *essentially* different from physical things; they are just different "frequencies" of the same spiritual force. These divisions are real only in the sense that they help us better understand ourselves and our world. In the final analysis, however, physical and mental realities are different ways of looking at the one force that is rooted in spirit.

Oneness of Time

One of the most challenging ways of looking at oneness concerns the concept of time. We've been brought up to think of time as linear, like a one-way street moving into the future. But is that the best model?

Many New Age teachings assert that time is nonexistent, an illusion created by our limited awareness. Cayce's readings, however, take a somewhat different point of view: They invite us to consider that past, present, and future are all connected.

You've probably had *experiences* that illustrate the unity of time, even if it's difficult to grasp the idea with your intellect. Perhaps you've had a dream that later came true. Events or situations in the dream became a physical reality weeks or months after you first perceived them. These "precognitive dreams" illustrate the oneness of time.

One woman dreamed of going up and down in an elevator in the company of Japanese men wearing three-piece suits. Upon awakening, she wrote down her dream and for weeks afterward tried to get a sense of its meaning. She speculated on the symbolism of elevators, Japanese men, and three-piece suits. She constructed some rather elaborate interpretations, but the time-bending quality wasn't evident until two years later, when she found herself traveling with an international trade show and events suddenly brought her old dream to mind. Leaving her room in a large Tokyo hotel, she headed to the restaurant for dinner. Suddenly she realized with a shock that she had spent several days going up and down in that elevator in the company of Japanese men wearing three-piece suits! Through the oneness of time, this woman "experienced" a situation two years before it actually happened.

Mystics from all cultures and all periods of history have contemplated this mysterious unity of time. To most rational intellects, however, yesterday seems completely removed from tomorrow. Exceptions come from the creative genius of people such as Albert Einstein—formulator of the theory of relativity—and Rupert Sheldrake, a modern-day biologist who argues persuasively in *The Presence of the Past* that invisible fields connect a living organism's past to both its present and its future.

Einstein also had some strong views on this subject. When one of his closest friends, Michele Besso, died in 1955, just four weeks before his own death, Einstein sent a letter of condolence to Besso's sister and son. In that letter he wrote, "Now he has departed from this strange world a little ahead of me. That means nothing. People like us, who believe in physics, know that the distinction between past, present, and future is only a stubbornly persistent illusion."

Sometimes the universe offers us a different kind of lesson about the unity of time. Consider this illustration of synchronicity, the term used by Carl Jung to describe simultaneous events that aren't caused by each other but seem to be meaningfully related.

A man was enjoying a birthday party thrown for him by his office colleagues. Suddenly, in the midst of the celebration, some movers appeared, wheeling in the man's new desk, which had been ordered several weeks earlier. The fact that his new desk arrived during his office birthday party was certainly not planned by anyone, yet the happy coincidence added meaningfully to his celebration. It was almost as if time itself had coordinated the two events through its innate oneness.

Oneness of Space

One of the best demonstrations of the oneness of space is Cayce's own psychic work. Twice a day for many years he put himself into a sleeplike altered state of consciousness and perceived information about people who were hundreds of miles away. Often the information concerned an individual's health, in which case Cayce described physical conditions in great detail even though his eyes were closed and the person was nowhere nearby.

Occasionally, as he began a reading, Cayce would make parenthetical comments about the person's environment, clothing, or activity. "Nice paintings on the wall," he'd say, or, "Loud red pajamas"—clairvoyant comments that were later verified. To one person who was just exiting from the door of his home in a different city, Cayce said, "Come back here and sit down!" Because he was experiencing all this from a level of awareness that emphasized the oneness of space, Cayce perceived and spoke as though he were right in the same room with the man.

Oneness of God and Humanity

At its center, the concept of oneness asserts that God is unified with humanity and that humanity is one with itself. After the mind-bending issues of energy, time, and space, this statement may seem easier to accept, yet for some people it is the most difficult aspect of oneness.

Throughout the ages, a long-standing theological argument poses the following problem: Is God "out there," somewhere far off and removed (transcendent), or is God "right here" within us and within all creation (immanent)? The law of oneness supports the "immanent" side of this debate, but many people find that hard to accept.

The primary stumbling block concerns how we see our enemies. If we assert that God is within us, then we are forced to conclude that God is in our adversaries as well, whoever they may be at the moment. If certain individuals or even complete segments of humanity are hard to accept, then it's difficult to believe that God is one with all of humanity. We may sometimes find ourselves thinking, Yes, God is one with all of humanity—except the Muslims, or the Russians, or the Democrats, or the Republicans, or my brother-in-law, or my supervisor.

If God is immanent in all creation, God is the thread that binds all of humanity together. Visionaries throughout history have recognized this. One example, from an occurrence in 1872, concerns a nine-year-old Native American boy from the Oglala Sioux nation who fell sick. During his illness, this boy, named Black Elk, had a mystical vision that initiated him on the path of becoming a shaman and healer for his tribe. At the climax of this vision (which he finally shared with a historian in the 1930s), he described being taken to the center of the world and shown the interconnectedness of all people and things. He speaks of this climactic moment, in *Black Elk Speaks:* "And while I stood there I saw more than I can tell and I understood more than I saw; for I was seeing in a sacred manner the shapes of all things in the spirit, and the shape of all shapes as they must live together like one being. And I saw that the sacred hoop of my people was one of many hoops that made one circle, wide as daylight and as starlight, and in the center grew one mighty flowering tree to shelter all the children of one mother and one father. And I saw that it was holy.''

What about Individuality and Uniqueness?

Individuality is a two-edged sword. We want to be free and independent, yet we know there's another side to this. Something in each of us longs for a sense of oneness. But individuality can turn into isolation, and isolation into loneliness. When we feel threatened or depressed, there is a natural craving for support from others. When we're feeling alone, it's difficult to recognize an invisible oneness that binds us to the rest of the universe. Quite naturally, we look for a *tangible* sense of community.

Shortly after crawling into bed, a five-year-old girl called out to her mother, who came quickly. The daughter explained that she missed the companionship of her younger brother, who usually shared the room with her. He was visiting their grandparents overnight. The girl had discovered that she was frightened to be left alone in the dark room. The mother tried to comfort the child. ''Don't be afraid, honey,'' she said. ''You know that you're surrounded by angels that love you and protect you. Now, don't you think that you can go to sleep knowing that they're by your bed keeping you safe?''

''No!'' the little girl insisted. ''I want something with hair and skin on it!''

This kind of desire for *concrete* connections with others spans all age groups. Not only children but adults as well want to counterbalance the freedom of individuality with the bonds of togetherness.

But the need for balance works the other way, too. Some people are understandably restless with the idea of oneness if it means a loss of individuality. Many Westerners are suspicious of the Oriental version of heaven known as *nirvana*.

Eastern poets have described human souls as drops of water that will ultimately dissolve into the ocean of God. This is not a comforting thought! Who wants to be a dissolved droplet losing forever one's unique and individual character? But maybe we've misinterpreted these metaphorical images that have arisen from Hinduism and Buddhism.

One spiritual teacher who has tried to help us understand Eastern philosophical concepts of oneness and individuality is Lama Anagarika Govinda. Describing himself as "an Indian national of European descent [born in Germany in 1898] and Buddhist faith," Govinda wrote his first book on Buddhism at the age of eighteen. Until his death in 1986 he spent his life interpreting for the West the wisdom of the East. He took the image of nirvana and turned it around. Rather than imagining that someday one's droplet of individuality will be dissolved into the universal oneness, he suggested, why not consider enlightenment as the universal, oceanic oneness being incorporated *into* each individual soul? So instead of the drop finally returning to the sea, it is all the qualities of the sea that enter into the drop.

The Cayce readings also do a marvelous job of illustrating and helping to resolve this conflict between individuality and universality. Our destiny as souls is reunion with God. Fulfilling our potential for spiritual evolution, we will know ourselves to be ourselves—that is, totally self-aware as individuals yet at the same time one with the whole—not *the* whole, but one *with the* whole.

Simultaneous individuality and universality sounds paradoxical. We can understand this concept better by examining the composition of a musical chord. When three notes blend harmoniously, they form a new entity—a chord. The notes don't lose their individuality, yet at the same time they merge into something far greater than their single identities. As we listen, our perception of the chord overshadows that of the unique tones, although the distinct notes still sound if we want to hear them. This resembles the experience we will have when we reach spiritual enlightenment. We won't lose a sense of individual identity, but it will be overshadowed by something even greater—an experience of our connections with everything.

Creating Your Future?

How does the principle of oneness relate to the way you shape your future? The concept of unity is intriguing and may even help you develop greater peace of mind. But how can you make practical use of this idea to create a personal future that is brighter and more fulfilling? Here are four ways in which you can learn to operate from the perspective of oneness and creatively build your own destiny.

First, seeing the oneness of time, you can realize that the resources needed for building a brighter future are at hand *today*. True, you may not have everything you want or even need for the entire journey, but you have the means to begin. Recall the parable of the mustard seed. It's the smallest of seeds, but over time it grows into the greatest of herbs. Do your best with what you have in hand. Cosmic law promises that as you do, more will be given.

Second, remembering that there is only one force in the universe, you can recognize that the energy you expend worrying about your future is something you can use in a more creative, constructive way. Consider the story of the worrywart executive whose secretary came in one day to discover him pacing fretfully back and forth in his office. When she asked him what was wrong, he barked, "Oil stock is plunging!" Perplexed, the secretary commented, "But sir, you don't have any oil stock." Frantically he replied, "But what if I did?"

How you use the one universal energy is up to you. Are you going to waste it on worry and regret, or will you apply your physical, mental, and spiritual energy with an eye toward constructive possibilities?

Third, recognizing the oneness of humanity, you will discover that the best way to help yourself is to help others. Repeatedly Edgar Cayce gave the same advice to individuals who were fearful or beset with troubles: Find people even less fortunate than yourself and do something to help them. This advice wasn't just an exercise in humility or kindheartedness. Cayce was helping individuals operate according to spiritual law. Jesus taught the same message: "Give, and it will be given to you . . . the measure . . . you give, will be the measure you get back" (Luke 6:38).

Fourth, feeling your oneness with the universe, you can see that your life situation, no matter how modest, has in miniature all the great opportunities, challenges, and themes of the human drama. Sometimes it's tempting to think that only the privileged few get the opportunity to experience the full range of human potential, but that's not true. Kings and hoboes have the same size dreams at night. Their fears and hopes are equally intense. There are no small parts in the tragicomic pageant of life.

An example from modern science illustrates how even a small part can contain all the richness and complexity of the whole. A photographic technique called holography uses laser light passing through a photographic plate to create a three-dimensional picture. If you've ever seen a holographic image, you know how remarkable it is. Yet even more astounding is the fact that if you cut this plate into pieces, *each piece* can also project a perspective of a full three-dimensional image. In the same way, you are a microcosm of the universe. Your joys, sorrows, hopes, challenges, and accomplishments are a miniature replica of all that happens in the universe.

EXERCISE

This exercise involves first the nurturance of a certain outlook on life, then specific efforts to transform some aspect of your life situation by using the principle of oneness.

First, begin to look at your life more often from the perspective of oneness. Recognize how your living situation, no matter how grand or humble, includes miniature versions of the great themes of the human journey, for example, the quest for meaning, the search for love, the paradoxical inner demands for both freedom and bonding. See the principle of oneness in the way your microcosmic life condition is a replica of the macrocosm.

Then, with this fresh, appreciative point of view, apply the concept of oneness more consciously than you have in the past. For example, pick one attitude or emotion that wastes energy and try to give that same energy a new, more positive expression. Remember that it's the same, the one energy resource of your life.

Or select an irritating, aggravating person and change the nature of your relationship. A good way to start is to try relating to aspects of that person where you *do* see similarities or common bonds.

Live for a Purpose
Greater than Yourself

"What's in it for me?" This has become a frequent question—even a mantra—for modern civilization. Almost everywhere you look you can find this motive operating. Television commercials tell us to "look out for number one" or encourage us to buy certain products because "I'm worth it." The scramble for personal advancement and the unrest it creates are dramatized continually on the daytime and evening soaps. Their call to arms is "Do unto others before they do unto you!"

Is this an expression of our real nature? At the center of our being are we beasts of prey operating only from the primal law of nature—survival of the fittest? Or are we sparks from the Creative Force, whose nature it is to give and love, to seek harmony, balance, and healing for all parts of creation?

Some would say that the jury is still out on this question. Others would say that the question itself is naive, that the human race appears to be made up of self-seeking splinters warring constantly among themselves and with their environment. But you have to be careful when looking at the evidence. Notice the major trends that define human nature but examine also the small, personal examples that often go unnoticed by the world at large.

One man recounted a childhood memory that had forever shaped his impression of human character. He had grown up in traditional, small-town U.S.A. As was typical, he earned his spending money by delivering newspapers in his neighborhood. In the early sixties it was customary for paperboys to go from customer to customer once a week and collect the weekly delivery fee.

One October evening, during his collecting rounds, the boy knocked on the door of a neighbor a few houses down from his own home. The woman who lived there came to the door in tears. She spoke rather incoherently, but the boy was able to make out that she had just learned of the sudden death of one of her grown children. Being no more than twelve or so, the boy had no idea what to say or do. But when he returned home, he found his mother, who was busily working in the kitchen, and told her what had happened. Upon hearing the news, his mother immediately quit what she was doing, threw on her coat, and hurried over to the neighbor to provide company and solace. She didn't think about it; she didn't say, "Gosh, I should go comfort her, but what would I say?" She just went.

This story would never have made the evening news: "Woman drops everything and runs to the aid of a neighbor!" But to the boy, who had felt so incapable of action, this was a most impressive example of human compassion and self-lessness.

The Two Faces of Humankind

Religions and philosophies through the ages have struggled to define the relationship between the two opposing natures of humankind: the selfish, "me first" nature and the nature that places concern for another even before one's own safety. For example, in the pagan pantheon of the ancient Romans, there existed the two-faced god Janus—one head with two images facing in opposite directions. The very story of the Buddha's enlightenment centers on his overcoming the two demons of selfishness: fear and desire. The Christian Jesus overcame the world by offering himself in love and resisting the temptation to save his own life. It's this same Jesus who tells his followers, "No one can serve two masters" (Matthew 6:24).

The philosophy found in the Cayce readings replays the same theme. One proverb found in several variations throughout the readings says in effect that we approach the throne of grace leaning on the arm of another whom we have helped. One reading is even more emphatic, saying that no one gets to heaven unless he or she is leaning on such an arm. In other words, attitudes and actions based on a genuine concern for someone or something greater than yourself actually lead you to your ultimate destiny: identification with the Creative Force of the universe. This is your true self.

But this crown is won only at a price. It takes courage to free yourself from the prison of ego-centeredness, from the conviction that your good is based on someone else's loss or that life is, in essence, survival of the fittest.

Myth as Teacher

Mythologies throughout the world describe this heroic struggle. Every culture tells the story in its own way, but in every case the purpose in telling the myth is to awaken in the listener a set of values that goes beyond pure self-interest. The hero or heroine lives for a bigger purpose than self-concern.

For example, the Sumerian hero Gilgamesh suffered through a painful quest to win for humankind the sign of immortality, the plant "Never Grow Old." He risked many dangers, finally diving to the bottom of the sea to retrieve this gift. His quest failed, however, when his treasure was eaten by a serpent.

Prometheus was chained to a rock and tortured because he brought the gift of fire to the human race. His story is the classic theme of fire theft: In stealing fire from the gods and bestowing it upon humanity, he gave us the gift of civilization. Yet in so doing, he aroused the wrath of the gods and suffered their revenge.

In a modern rendition of this timeless theme, J. R. R. Tolkien's hobbit Frodo risked life and limb to undo the evil that was forged into a magic ring. His quest was to steal into the heart of the evil empire of Sauron and cast the ring into the volcanic furnace of Mount Doom. Only such an act could undo the plague of evil that was threatening to engulf Middle Earth.

In the psychic readings of Edgar Cayce a new mythology unfolds. Although its setting may seem fanciful, the themes illustrate brilliantly the struggle between being selfish and living for a greater purpose. To do this Cayce whisks us back to the lost continent of Atlantis. There, in the mists of prehistory, he describes an almost superhuman civilization divided into two opposing forces. On one side are the sons of Belial; on the other are the children of the Law of One. These two groups disagree on the fundamental issues of life. The sons of Belial can see no purpose in life other than self-aggrandizement and self-indulgence. The children of the Law of One, in contrast, conceive of life as an opportunity to measure up to the standards of caring and loving.

The chief focus of contention between these two groups was a third class of beings who were in a dulled state of consciousness. They were a type of subrace, souls who were trapped unconsciously in physical form. The sons of Belial wanted to keep these dulled, vulnerable beings in their inferior state and use them for slave labor. The children of the Law of One wanted to elevate the condition of these trapped souls and raise them to their full potential, to redeem them, as it were.

In this vivid myth Cayce illustrates the fundamental questions facing us today both as individuals and as members of the human race. Are we to live only for ourselves, using others to our advantage, or are we to care about someone or something beyond ourselves? The first choice may lead to greater comfort and convenience, at least temporarily. The second calls for the definite *inconvenience* of taking on the burdens of others. Yet the Cayce readings, the ancient mythologies, and the great world religions all agree that only the second choice leads to happiness.

Self versus Selfishness

One argument surfaces periodically, contending that all morality is based on selfishness. We've heard this assertion from the Greek sophists as well as from the philosophies set forth in such modern books as *Atlas Shrugged* and *The Fountainhead* by Ayn Rand. If doing a good deed makes you happy, the argument postulates, then you are doing it to be happy—and that action is indicative of a selfish motive. Therefore, being kind is no more virtuous than being cruel: both are done for the pleasant sensation they bring.

Such a point of view, however, fails to grasp the distinction between happiness and pleasure, between self and selfishness; it misses some of the depth of who we really are. If humanity is seen only as a complex physical organism, then the entire spectrum of human thought and action is reduced to biological terms. Happiness and pleasure become the same. However, if humanity is seen with a *spiritual* dimension, living *through* the physical but not limited to it, then the range of human potential is broadened immensely. Then we have a choice because happiness and pleasure are no longer identical. We *can* live from a purely physical perspective, forever pursuing pleasure and avoiding pain, *or* we can choose to live according to our *spiritual* selves, whose nature is to care deeply and compassionately for others, even to the extent of self-sacrifice.

In his thought-provoking book *Creative Brooding*, Richard Raines tells the story of a band of prisoners of war held captive in a Japanese prison camp during World War II. The prisoners are outside the camp doing construction work for their captors. When the work is finished, the shovels are counted, and one is missing. Furious, the captors insist that the shovel be returned and that the culprit who hid it reveal himself. The prisoners look at each other dumbly, which only infuriates the captors more. Finally, the guard in charge shouts, "All die, all die!!" and prepares for a general execution of the entire work party. Then one man steps forward and announces that he took the shovel. In a fit of rage, the head guard clubs the man to death with the butt of his rifle. The work party trudges back to camp, carrying the man's body and all the tools. When they arrive in the camp, the shovels are counted again. The first count had been in error; there never had been a missing shovel. Raines appends to this true story the biblical verse "No one has greater love than this, to lay down one's life for one's friends" (John 15:13).

Few of us are called upon to make such a heroic sacrifice. Yet every day in smaller ways we have opportunities to choose between serving only the self and serving a greater purpose.

What Purpose to Choose?

What is the purpose that we are called upon to serve? How do we choose among all the missions and causes that beckon us to join? How do we know which one is best?

One method for evaluating purposes is found in the phrase "You will know them by their fruits" (Matthew 7:16). In other words, does the purpose help create greater peace, content-ment, understanding, or love, or does it create strife, dissension, fear, or hatred? Does the cause contribute to the *common good*, or does it benefit a few at the expense of others?

These sorts of questions are found in the Cayce readings that stress the importance of living by ideals. Ideals are our motives—*why* we do something as opposed to *what* we do. In fact, one troubled person was told by Cayce that the most important thing *anyone* can do is set a spiritual ideal and then live by it.

From one point of view, there is only a single spiritual ideal for the human race, and your life can become an attempt to live according to it. But from another perspective, you have a very particular ideal, a mission with which you were born. It's a very specific purpose that no one else can fulfill as well as you can.

That common spiritual ideal is probably beyond neat definitions, but it's clearly about elevating the level or quality of existence for the human race and for all of creation. This might be called the "Great Work" or the "Great Purpose." However, we each have only our little part to play in that work. The trick is to remember that our part is important even when it seems small.

There is the story of a reporter who went to interview the builders of a New York skyscraper. He came to three masons all working at the same job in the same place and asked each what he was doing. The first replied, "I'm laying a brick." The second replied, "I'm building a wall." But the third replied, "I'm helping to build a monument that will be admired for centuries."

Is Living for a Purpose the Same as Joining a Group or Movement?

A purpose in life is certainly not the same as an organized cause or movement, yet often we find organizations or groups serving as *vehicles* for certain ideals or purposes. Joining a group or movement is often *part* of living for a purpose greater than pure self-interest. Yet caution is advised: Organized movements or groups can create a strong impression of love and peace *within the group* while wreaking havoc on unfortunate individuals not within its embrace. The Nazi party and the Ku Klux Klan are classic examples. As a member of such a group, one may have the impression that one is living for a greater purpose, yet that purpose is in fact destructive—a group ego responding to the ruthless call of nature's "survival of the fittest."

For a group or movement to be truly in tune with the Greater Purpose, it must reach out to the rest of humanity not merely for recruiting purposes but in genuine love and compassion.

The test of a group's attunement with the great ideal and purpose is whether its efforts result in a bettering of people in general.

The Two-Edged Sword

Even a casual observation of life shows that a person can't please everyone. It's impossible to perform any act without causing at least an inconvenience to someone else. For example, if you're committed to a cleaner environment and join efforts to shut down a polluting chemical plant, you contribute to the loss of the jobs and livelihoods of many honest, hard-working families.

Years ago a woman was traveling through the beautiful northern California area known as Big Sur. During one stop in the trip she asked some local people if they knew where the famous photographer and environmentalist Ansel Adams lived. She remembered that Adams had been very active in the campaign to protect this area from industrialization. The traveler got a firsthand lesson in the paradox of positive action when the local inhabitants told her that in their opinion Adams was not a hero but a meddler. She realized then that Adams presented a threat to these people and to their delicate local economy. They didn't care what impact they made on the environment for future generations—they only wanted their jobs and factories.

Begin Today and Make it Practical

Live for a purpose greater than yourself. Now, what can you do to apply this principle? Is there some major work to accomplish? Is there a certain group or organization that provides the perfect opportunity to serve the Great Purpose or Ideal? The answer, probably is, both yes and no.

It's important to feel part of the great work—the work of elevating the human condition physically, mentally, and spiritually. It's important and helpful to realize that this work is greater than any one person, lifetime, or even historical period. Broadening the scope of your purpose to include the past and the future connects you with the humanity that has gone before and that which is yet to come. Sometimes you may even feel a sense of awe at being part of something so big and important.

Yet at the same time, living your purpose must be a day-to-day and moment-to-moment experience. The great work is accomplished by the little things that are done from day to day, such as running next door to provide support and comfort to a grieving neighbor. It's taking time to help a child figure out a difficult math problem. It's being kind. It's responding to your world with compassion and acting accordingly.

EXERCISE

Do something today—probably just a small thing—from which you derive no personal benefit beyond the delight of doing it. This deed should bring you no direct financial reward, no attention or acclaim, perhaps not even words of grateful appreciation. The effort should, however, bring benefit to someone or something else: another individual or group of people, an animal, the environment, and so on.

From this one small action, take note of your inner responses. For example, in the process do you encounter resistance or fear? Finally, recognize how this way of acting—even with just some small effort—creates a feeling of connection with things greater than yourself.

Truth Is a Growing Thing

The challenge to recognize truth in the world around us is not new. Even in Cayce's time, which was not so far removed from our own, it was hard to know what one could believe in. Economic uncertainties, changing social values, and threats of war were at least as prevalent in the 1920s, 1930s, and 1940s as they are in these final years of the twentieth century. Just like us, the people who came to Cayce wanted desperately to be able to believe in something, to know the truth.

Some of those people needed more accurate descriptions of their physical ailments, problems that until then had only been *mis*diagnosed. Others wanted a more reliable understanding of vocational or interpersonal difficulties. Many came seeking facts about spiritual development. All of them probably sensed this one principle: We require truth in order to grow into a better future.

Western civilization is based largely on the importance of truth. Our legal system—the social contract that binds us as a people—is devoted to the twin ideals of truth and justice. Each witness in our courts must solemnly swear to be honest when offering testimony, promising to speak only the truth. The very symbol of our judicial system is that of a blindfolded woman carrying a scale. Thus, blind to preconceptions or vested interests, Lady Justice is able to pass judgment based solely on the impartial, objective scale of truth.

The scale of truth is an age-old symbol. According to the mysterious lore of the ancient Egyptians, at death each soul entered the judgment hall of Osiris, the Egyptian god who ruled the Abode of the Blessed (a place of paradise). All souls desired to enter the realm of Osiris because the rest of the underworld was inhabited by soul-devouring monsters.

However, not everyone was awarded entry. First, a soul had to proclaim its innocence of crime. As an individual entering the afterlife pleaded its case, its heart was weighed on a scale against the "feather of truth." If the heart was not truthful, the soul did not pass and the unhappy Egyptian faced a dreadful fate.

From that distant myth we can trace the ideal and pursuit of truth as it has marched through all the eras of human history. Unfortunately, this quest was sometimes sacrificed when it confronted a worldly power with its own biases. For example, in the sixteenth century Galileo was forced to recant his astronomical observations, truths he had ascertained with a new invention: the telescope. The Catholic Church found his ideas threatening and was prepared to send the scientific pioneer to an early death. Hundreds of years later the Nazi regime ridiculed Einstein's theory of relativity and eventually put a price on the scientist's head. But today Einstein's theory is universally accepted as scientific truth. The Church, too, recently reversed its condemnation of Galileo, in effect admitting its error.

What Is Truth?

This philosophical riddle has puzzled the mind since humanity first developed the ability to think and question. Sometimes, however, the question has been posed not by sincere seekers but by doubters. For example, Jesus said to Pontius Pilate, "I came into the world to bear witness to truth. Everyone who belongs to the truth listens to my voice." Pilate asked him, "What is truth?" (John 18:37–38), but he then showed his own cynical bias by failing to wait for an answer. Instead he hurriedly concerned himself with the functions of his office, and the answer was not forthcoming. Cayce pointed out that because of Pilate's impatience the world lost a great opportunity to understand the truth more fully.

Rather than wait for a wise man or woman to pronounce the truth, contemporary seekers turn to *scientific inquiry* for validation. Ideas once articulated by Galileo and Einstein are now accepted because they have been proved by repeated observation and hold up to controlled experimentation. Such an approach has proved to be highly effective in identifying *physical* truth. But the human soul thrives in realms beyond the material. We need to be equally diligent in investigating other kinds of questions:

How can we determine the truth of a human heart?

What values and characteristics are most true to the human spirit?

What is our true mission on the earth?

These questions are elusive and also susceptible to criticism. As soon as we move beyond the physical domain, it becomes tempting to say, "It's all subjective! Every person must arrive at his or her own answers."

A youth was confronted with these more subtle questions of truth one sleepy afternoon during a high school English class. He was asked to read a piece of romantic poetry, and the words flowed together easily as he recited the poem aloud. The sense of the poem was this: While sitting underneath a tall oak tree, the poet had felt the presence of God. The poem was merely a tribute to the beauty of the tree and its Creator. No one in the class had felt very inspired by this poetic reading, and it had done little to dissipate the lethargy of that long schoolday afternoon.

Then the teacher posed a very unusual question to the class. "Is the poem true?" he asked. He proceeded to orchestrate a marvelous Socratic dialogue with his students, exploring the nature of truth. Skillfully he steered his young minds on a collision course with the question, "Can a poet sitting under a tree discover truth just as readily as a scientist can?"

At first the class was quick to say no. Then the young man who had read the poem aloud—who had perhaps experienced it more deeply that afternoon than his classmates had—conceded, "Maybe the poet can find truth, but there's no way to test it, so we can never be sure."

But the words that lodged permanently in the youth's mind were his teacher's closing remarks. "Just remember," the teacher said, "there are other means to truth besides the laboratory!" For the young man, that afternoon's English class became a rare mind-expanding episode that helped influence his life's direction, for he'd been confronted with a new question.

If truth is more than just provable fact, then what is it?

Truth Is a Growing Thing

Many people wrestling with these same questions came to Edgar Cayce for answers. Often his readings defined truth as "a growing thing." There are two ways to interpret this rather poetic definition. One is that truth itself is forever changing. Yesterday's truth is different from today's, which will in turn be different from tomorrow's.

Unfortunately, this kind of relativism can lead to sophistry. The sophists were ancient Greek philosophers who argued that all truths, including values, are relative and therefore meaningless. For them the very quest for truth and value was also meaningless. Obviously this attitude is not what Cayce intended. As we change and develop, certain truths become more *relevant* than others. But in spite of this flexible approach, Cayce always insisted that truth "is indeed ever the same."

A second interpretation recognizes that truth is a growing thing because it *generates growth*. As an analogy, one might say that lawn fertilizer is a "growing thing." However, the fertilizer itself doesn't grow: it *promotes* growth.

The Cayce philosophy focuses more on this second interpretation. Truth is the divinely inspired *impulse toward growth*, moving each soul toward the fulfillment of its destiny, even though truth can sometimes make one uncomfortable. But that's the way growth works. To change and develop often means to be *stretched*. The old ways do not surrender easily; they resist when accepting the truth requires a new outlook or a new way of acting.

Yet despite the discomfort that may accompany truth, something in us *wants* and *appreciates* it. For example, think about your deepest friendships. Aren't they the ones in which truth and honesty flow freely? Isn't your best friend the one who can tell you the truth even when it makes one or both of you uncomfortable? In close relationships the commitment is to each other's growth, and even when the truth hurts, it can be offered with loving support.

How Can We Recognize Truth?

Many wars have been fought over the issue of truth. Consider, for example, seventeenth-century Europe, which Joseph Campbell characterizes as "a world of madmen flinging the Bible at one another—French Calvinists, German Lutherans, Spanish and Portuguese inquisitors, Dutch rabbis and miscellaneous others . . ." (*Creative Mythology*). In the midst of this free-for-all religious war, Benedict Spinoza, a Jewish philosopher, boldly affirmed that God's truth can be found not in a book but in the human heart and mind. His words were condemned at the time as having been forged in hell by a renegade Jew and the devil.

A more current example of the mad war over truth may be found in the city of Beirut, where Christians, Muslims, and Jews continue to slaughter one another, each in the name of the same God.

In such an impassioned and cacophonous world, how can you hope to get a sense of the truth Cayce described in his readings—the kind that will help you grow and build a healthy future?

Fortunately, there is a way to determine truth. As a growing thing, it generates attitudes and actions that are constructive. In other words, jealousy, malice, hatred, and backbiting are not the fruits of the spirit of truth. If these characteristics are present, then the person, group, or movement that displays them has lost the spirit of truth regardless of its slogans, banners, or doctrine.

The spirit of truth generates patience, love, fellowship, and kindness, for these attitudes tend to build up rather than tear down. What's more, they build things that are lasting. When truth is active, growth is irrepressible, with sometimes amazing results.

The power of living for truth is illustrated in the story of Jaime Escalante, whose work was made known to millions by the popular movie *Stand and Deliver*. In 1982 he began teaching mathematics in Garfield High School. At that time the school—characterized by violence, vandalism, and an appalling scholastic record—was a genuine microcosm of the social dilemmas plaguing the barrios of East Los Angeles.

Escalante took on the challenge of raising the performance level at the school. Many times he had to be firm, and he had to commit to what he saw as truth in education. His primary tools for living that truth were enthusiasm, encouragement, and a genuine love for his students. By the end of the year, eighteen members of his top class passed the advanced placement calculus exam, one of the toughest mathematics tests in the country; in fact, they passed with such flying colors that the testing authorities suspected cheating. Only when the students were tested a second time was their extraordinary achievement acknowledged. One teacher's commitment to truth as he saw it produced extraordinary growth in the lives of many teenagers. And this pattern actually increased in the years that followed: In 1987, a total of eighty-seven students passed the difficult calculus test.

Power of the Lie

Unfortunately, the kind of noble truth exemplified in the work of Jaime Escalante is not manifested everywhere with such purity. As Cayce sometimes put it, even though the truth always derives from one source, souls with free will can manipulate that truth into half-truths, which become lies. In fact, in the material world the influence of *lying* is very strong. The ancient Persian prophet Zoroaster understood this power when he named the force of evil Angra Mainyu, which means "the Deceiver."

What is a lie? It's an action or a word (or even silence itself) that accompanies the intention to deceive. Often this deliberate deception is practiced in order to gain power over another. In 1938, as Hitler was simultaneously persecuting Jews and building up his war machine, Albert Einstein published an article in *Collier's* magazine entitled "Why Do They Hate the Jews?" The article began with the following ancient fable:

A shepherd boy said to a horse, "You are the noblest beast that treads the earth. You deserve to live in untroubled bliss. And you would enjoy that fate if it weren't for that treacherous stag. He and his kind are deliberately stealing from you what is rightfully yours. His faster pace allows him to get to the water holes before you. He and his tribe drink up all the water, while you and your children are left to thirst. Allow me to lead you," said the shepherd boy, "and I will deliver you from your unjust and threatening situation."

The horse, blinded by his own hatred and envy, yielded to the lad's bridle. Thus he lost his freedom and became a slave.

Einstein used this parable to illustrate the power and purpose of lies. The shepherd boy represented the group or clique that used flattery and accusation to gain power over the German people, symbolized by the horse. The stag, in Einstein's story, represented the Jews. However, any person or group can play the role of scapegoat. In other words, the stag represents the victim of the lie. But the perpetrators of the lie are both the shepherd boy *and the horse*! The boy whispers the words, but the horse allows his envy and fear to compel him to accept the lie as truth. In continuing his article, Einstein warns that each of us has played the part of the horse at one time or another and that we are in constant danger of playing it again.

Lying is not something we do only to each other; we also lie to ourselves. Sometimes we practice self-deception through delusions about our own importance. Other times we rationalize our behavior, blaming anyone (or anything) else for our problems because we don't want to take responsibility for what happens to us. We see ourselves as innocents, while evil guys proliferate in our imagination. Whenever we're in this frame of mind, we can be sure that we're listening to a whispered lie and playing the part of the horse in Einstein's parable.

What a Tangled Web

In the long run, lying never succeeds. According to the Cayce material, only truth has permanence: it alone is eternal, while everything born of falsehood is destined to pass away. Deceit, whether to ourselves or to others, always catches up with us eventually. That universal law is captured in the aphorism "O what a tangled web we weave,/ When first we practise to deceive." Or, put in a more positive way: Always tell the truth, and you'll never have to worry about your memory.

Lying is hard on the mind and body; it takes a toll. While truth is a growing thing, lies are destructive, warping the mind and even the physical body. The popular fairy tale of Pinocchio touches on this danger. Every time Pinocchio told a lie, his nose would lengthen. In other words, a heavy diet of lying actually shapes a person's physiognomy (as when we speak of shifty eyes or a dishonest face).

There is a story about Abraham Lincoln trying to fill an appointment to an important government post. His advisers had selected a man who seemed to fill the bill perfectly. After listening to an impressive list of qualifications, Lincoln rejected the man, saying, "I don't like his face." Exasperated, his advisers said, "Mr. President, a man can't choose his face!" Lincoln replied, "Gentlemen, I disagree. By the time a man is forty, he's responsible for his face!" The point here, obviously, is not one of physical beauty but of character, which Lincoln believed could be perceived in one's facial expression.

See the Truth by Being the Truth

Truth is not a commodity that you discover and then stick in your purse or pocket, nor is it for sale on the open market. *Knowing the truth is possible only when one lives as truthfully as possible.* In practical terms, this means just one thing: Tell the truth; be honest.

No doubt exceptions to this rule come to mind. You can probably think of a hypothetical situation where it seems best to lie in order to save a life, spare someone's feelings, or further a high-minded cause. But don't get too caught up in imagined circumstances. What would happen if you spoke and acted truthfully in every one of your real-life situations? Of course, you may need to be *tactful* and *sensitive* with your words and deeds. But if you'll look carefully at each situation, you're likely to find that truth will deliver the best results in the long run. Honesty will provide growth.

This is sound advice from the Cayce material. However, it isn't always easy to recognize how to live it. Life often brings difficult tests. For example, suppose you face this kind of real-life dilemma: It's a hot, sticky summer evening, and you're exhausted as you wait in line at a major airport terminal. You're returning on a Sunday from a weeklong trip, really looking forward to Monday as a day of recuperation at home before returning to work on Tuesday.

But something is amiss. The flight is overbooked, and when you get to the check-in counter, you're informed that many passengers with reservations won't be able to get on the flight. Priority will be given to those who really must get to their destinations because of commitments for Monday morning. Then the question from the gate attendant is addressed to you: Do you have to be at work on Monday, or can you give up your seat and fly out tomorrow?

How should you respond? Do you tell the literal truth or slip in a "little white lie" that ensures your seat on the flight for Sunday evening? What does it mean to be honest in a situation like this one? Is it possible to be truthful with the facts while being dishonest about your authentic needs?

There is no easy answer to a quandary like this. Each person must decide what would be the most truthful thing to do. Whether or not you're an airline traveler, you probably face hard choices like this one quite regularly. Questions of truth confront us continually. What is true, genuine, and reliable in the world around us? And what does it really mean to be truthful and honest to oneself? Perhaps the best principle to keep in mind as we make these decisions is that truth is a growing thing. Be willing to live truthfully, even though the growth of truth may sometimes stretch you and make you uncomfortable.

EXERCISE

Live one entire day as truthfully as you can. Catch yourself if you start to exaggerate in conversation with people. This temptation to lie may be strongest in your relationship with *yourself*. Make a special effort to achieve internal honesty: Don't mask your needs or intentions. Speak and act with tact and sensitivity but attempt to be as honest as possible.

Be truthful with *yourself*. For example, in your own mind, avoid blaming others for your difficulties. At the same time, eliminate deceitful statements that you may silently express to yourself, words that deny your authentic talents and self-worth.

Watch for the growth that happens as you try to live truthfully.

| PRINCIPLE #7 |

Evil Is Just Good Gone Wrong

It is time for the evening news. With a mixture of curiosity and trepidation you turn on the television. What else could have happened today in this crazy modern society? During the next half hour you hear a few uplifting stories, but most of the program is devoted to pain, anger, and suffering. Violence, addiction, warfare—even the more covert but equally disheartening white-collar crime—are described.

How do you respond to this negative input? One way, of course, is to turn off the television set and not think about the news. There's something to be said for this approach, since fretting may only add negative mental energy (yours) to these ills. A constant barrage of disturbing information can easily lead to worry, fear, or despair. However, ignoring evil doesn't make it disappear.

Not all negative influences are as dramatic and destructive as the bad news we receive from the media. For example, many of us must deal with such challenges in our families and businesses and our community relationships. Deceit, coercion, and greed are difficult themes in almost everyone's life, and the struggle isn't just outside ourselves. We wrestle with destructive traits *inside* as well. These challenges are so close to home that they won't go away just by switching off the TV. How do we handle these unavoidable encounters with negative influences?

All of us deal with this dilemma almost daily. It was no different for Edgar Cayce. In February 1931 Cayce and his friends saw his lifelong dream of a hospital fall from reality to foreclosure with the stock market crash. The hospital had been an extraordinary accomplishment, a place where people were treated by physicians and nurses exactly as their individualized Cayce health readings instructed. Along with the financial collapse, personal dissension among several of the founders ended this medical novelty after just three years.

For a while Cayce felt that his whole life was falling apart. In November of the same year he (along with his wife and secretary) was arrested in New York City, indicted for violating a city ordinance forbidding fortune-telling. The whole event was traumatic, and although all three were acquitted, the shock and embarrassment were severe. Worse, there were reasons to suspect that the entire incident was an act of vindictiveness by a former friend.

During this period Cayce's readings for himself warned that he was losing the will to live. If something wasn't done, he would shortly die. With this warning in mind, Cayce's friends rallied around him and chose a new initiative. They asked for and received a special series of readings on spiritual development. Even if there no longer was a Cayce Hospital, they reasoned, Cayce himself possessed vast inner resources that could still be used to help many other people. The effort succeeded, and rather than conclude this incarnation, Cayce renewed his spirits and persevered. The set of readings directed especially to this group between 1931 and 1942 provided a systematic philosophy of spiritual growth. His friends had responded creatively to the discouraging negativity of 1931, and out of their efforts came material that is generally considered to be among the best Cayce ever produced.

One of the most challenging perspectives suggested in those readings concerns the nature of evil. In short, Cayce proposed a radical view of negative influences: that evil is simply good gone wrong, that embedded in the worst evil is an original impulse for good. This philosophy entails a willingness to meet conditions head on—no avoidance, no retreat, no flipping off the TV out of dismay. Evil is no illusion: it's real. However, we usually don't understand its essential nature.

In one reading the following puzzle is articulated: Which is the greater reality, the love of God manifested in the Christ or the *essence* of love that resides hidden in the vilest passion? A surprising answer is offered: The two realities are one and the same! Even the worst human behavior has within it the disguised seed of truth and love. The reading finally concluded by stating that ungodliness was "just under" godliness—in other words, very near.

Three Views of Evil

Philosophers throughout history have struggled to reckon with evil while continuing to believe in the essential goodness of the universe. In his book *People of the Lie*, psychiatrist M. Scott Peck divides the different ways of looking at evil into three categories, each of which has its own contingent of believers.

One way to deal with evil is to deny its reality. Through metaphysical sleight of hand, evil is dismissed as a figment of the human imagination. This view contends that evil is just an illusion, part of a bigger mistake that humans usually make when they believe in duality (separation between God and humanity). According to this philosophy, evil is simply an aspect of what the Hindus call *maya*—the complex world revealed to us by our senses which conceals the deeper unity of all life.

Those who deny the reality of evil may try to overcome it by detaching themselves from the material world altogether. They may try to rise above all desires or fears that are part of the physical life and strive for a level of consciousness that transcends the duality of good and evil. Their objective is nirvana, an inner state of blissful oneness. Peck cites Christian Science and the New Age material *A Course in Miracles* as modern, Western expressions of this theory.

In the Middle Eastern land of Persia, there emerged a counterview—a second philosophy—that the entire universe is locked in violent combat between the two opposing forces of good and evil. Peck labels this perspective "diabolical dualism." The first to articulate this approach was the mysterious prophet Zarathustra (or Zoroaster to the Greeks). Exactly when he lived is not certain, but by the sixth century B.C. his philosophy had been thoroughly absorbed into the Persian religion.

Whereas the first perspective on evil might encourage a person to withdraw into a special state of consciousness, the second, embodied in Zoroaster's ideas, calls for action: each person is duty-bound to combat evil wherever it's found. And the battle may be waged anywhere—against an enemy nation, another person, or even within oneself. The devil is loose and must be vanquished.

Diabolical dualism, with its insistence on an independent, powerful force called evil, is expressed in many modern doctrines—fundamentalism in the Christian and Muslim worlds, for example. Peck himself admits to favoring this position, which can motivate believers to work tirelessly against such evils as poverty, ignorance, and oppression.

However, the same spirit can be seen at work in the horrible deeds of the Spanish Inquisition or the McCarthy hearings of the 1950s. Ironically, this same "fight for the right" zealotry can have results directly opposite to those intended, creating more fervor and compassion toward what is being opposed.

A third view of evil, defined by Peck as "integrative dualism," most closely resembles Cayce's perspective and takes a middle ground between the other two. Evil is real, this philosophy asserts, but is part of something bigger, integrated with goodness in such a way that spiritual growth is possible. In this manner, so-called evil can actually be a blessing to the seeker, by making available a series of distinct moral choices with which to exercise one's free will. The Jewish philosopher Martin Buber illustrated this school of thought with an analogy about baking bread. Evil is like the yeast in dough, he said. When we deal with it properly, using a loving will, it can create an expansion of the soul.

We are called to do something *about* evil: to transform it. In the language of the Cayce readings, the transformation of evil begins with finding the essence of its goodness.

The integrative view of evil combines elements from the other two models. Sometimes we must stand up against evil, confront it directly. Then again, the individual human mind plays a large role in what we see as evil; we must recognize clearly the evil within *ourselves* before we can see it objectively in the *outside* world. Cayce taught this time and again to those who came for readings and claimed that they were beset by hindering, evil forces. All that you can know of evil, he reminded them, must first be met within yourself.

The Parable of the Ax and the Tree

Rudolf Steiner was a contemporary of Edgar Cayce. Born in Austria in 1861, Steiner became one of the most influential spiritual teachers of the early twentieth century and made tremendous contributions to society in terms of his spiritual approach to medicine, agriculture, the arts, and education. Steiner demonstrated the use of art, music, and drama in the awakening of the soul. Just before World War I, Steiner wrote, directed, and produced four extraordinary plays about spiritual development. In one of these Mystery Dramas he addressed the question of evil with an instructive parable.

There was once a man who was troubled with the question of evil. Everything came from God, he reasoned, and since God must be only good, where did evil come from? The man struggled long and hard with this question but was unable to discover the answer. One day he heard a conversation between an ax and a tree. The ax was boasting to the tree, "I can cut you down, but you have no such power over me!" To this haughty ax, the tree answered, "A year ago a man came to me and cut from my body a wooden branch which now makes your handle. So you see, your very ability to cut me down derives from the power I have given you."

When the man heard this conversation, he was struck with an insight about how evil is rooted in good.

In this little fable Steiner clearly articulated his view on the question of evil, one that is consistent with Cayce's. Evil is real, not merely an illusion. However, its very energy is rooted in the one good Creative Force—God. Therefore, it's impossible to destroy evil. To conquer it, one must transform it. The first step in the transformation process is to see the kernel of goodness from which it springs.

How to See the Essential Goodness within a Fault

Looking for a nucleus of good within something bad may seem like an unrealistic challenge. Instead of trying to see essential goodness in a heinous crime, try a more modest effort. Suppose you perceive a fault in your friend—for example, he talks too much. Every time you're in a conversation with him, you find you have to cut him off or he'll continue to bend your ear forever. Using the integrated dualism model, how can you deal with this annoying behavior?

First, acknowledge to yourself how you feel. Be honest: you consider his habitual behavior to be bad. Honesty is important, particularly when trying first to meet evil within ourselves. In fact, Peck describes *deception* as a fundamental quality of evil. Evil is essentially dishonest—the force behind lying.

Next, look deeper. Look for the original impulse that is good, even though that impulse has been twisted into a fault. You may need to practice this step for a while before you are successful. Begin with speculation. What might be the essence of goodness in your garrulous, annoying friend? His habit of talking excessively may be rooted in a desire to have friends, and it's admirable to desire friendship. Maybe he erroneously believes that talking demonstrates his friendliness, that the more he talks, the more he will be liked. Perhaps something deep within him knows that communication and dialogue are valuable. That seed of truth may not have been immediately obvious to you when his nonstop talking was such an irritation. Or maybe he genuinely wants to help other people by sharing his knowledge and experience. The compulsive chatter masks an authentic desire to give.

The third step in the process is to try to understand *how* this initial impulse for good is being twisted into a fault. From our example, perhaps the excessive talking behavior is being *exaggerated* by fear. Maybe your friend fears being unpopular, so he tries too hard to make conversation. Or maybe an essential truth is being expressed in an outer way exclusively, missing the inner application. For example, in his concern for communication and dialogue, your friend may have forgotten the need for *inner* dialogue with the spirit. His overly talkative nature is thus an imbalanced expression of an essential truth.

So what do you do once you've acknowledged the fault, seen its essential goodness, and come to understand how it's getting distorted? First, allow this insight to alter your attitude toward your friend. Once you think differently about this person, surprising changes may happen in you and in him. You may find his conversations less annoying because you are sympathetic and understand him better. Your new attitudes toward him (when you're together *and* apart) may trigger a change in his behavior.

Seeing the Essential Goodness in Your Own Fault

As Cayce and the other proponents of integrated dualism suggest, the question of evil eventually comes around to this principle: To overcome evil in the world, we must first transform its portion in ourselves. None of us can say with honest conviction, "I have no faults." Although we may be painfully aware of our shortcomings, we often don't have any idea what to do about them. When contemplating our own destructive qualities, most of us usually get stuck in guilt, a paralyzing emotion.

Guilt puts you at war with yourself. When one part of you fails to live up to a standard you hold, another part points an imaginary finger of condemnation. This internal warfare can create psychological and even physical ill health.

How can you deal with such shortcomings in a responsible and compassionate way? Remember that the law of essential goodness applies to you as well. Bad is simply good gone wrong. Each of your faults is the by-product of some essential truth or seed of goodness that has gotten distorted, overdone, or twisted in a selfish way. Each is redeemable if you don't let self-condemnation and guilt keep you from reclaiming that essential goodness. However, *this is not a clever rationalization to let you off the hook*. Faults are faults, and you'll need to do something about them. But there's hope. The negative qualities in you contain something that can be transformed, something that can express itself in a beautiful, constructive way.

The following story illustrates how a young career woman was able to see through one of her faults and find again the original strength from which it grew. One year she received an astrology book for her birthday. As many people might do, she opened it first to the general description of her own sun sign. She was a Virgo, born in September. Eagerly she read what sort of personality the stars indicated she had. However, after reading the synopsis, she felt very disappointed. Virgos seemed to be rather unpleasant people, finicky and very critical of others. The book even included a humorous "Virgo Prayer" that read, "Lord, please make us perfect—and don't mess it up like you did the last time!"

Although she appreciated the humor in this prayer, she began to think of times when she had been very critical. These memories led to further recollections, and soon she was convinced that her personality fault was rooted mainly in criticism. At first this realization depressed her. Any time she had a thought or observation that even suggested a criticism, she would reprimand herself for being so judgmental.

Finally she voiced her distress to her husband. In tears, she revealed to him the negative thoughts that had been plaguing her. Rather absentmindedly, her husband said, "Honey, you just care enough to want things to be done right. There's nothing wrong with that!"

These casual words helped the woman get a new perspective on her dilemma. She realized that there was an essential goodness in her tendency toward judgmental criticism. Of course, the character trait still needed some work. Nevertheless, she now saw a possibility to unlock a wonderful character strength so that it could express itself clearly and without distortion. With this hopeful feeling, she again reviewed moments from her past when she remembered being critical. Sure enough, some of the memories did seem to center on a desire to make conditions better. However, she realized that on other occasions her initial impulse was distorted by insecurity or unresolved feelings toward a person.

Next, she tried to observe herself in the very act of being critical. Sometimes, she noticed, she would use her discriminating mind to seize control of a situation or reinforce a negative attitude about someone. At other times, however, she realized that in being critical she was simply striving for quality control.

Eventually this woman came to realize that her innate sense of discrimination was a strength, not a weakness. Recognizing the essential goodness in this trait helped her feel better about herself. At the same time, she learned to catch any impulses to use her gift for negative or selfish purposes. She had learned a spiritual truth: Embedded in any fault is a seed of goodness.

In the months that followed she was able more frequently to express her desire to make things better in ways that weren't misshaped by other emotions. Although the changes came slowly, she steadily transformed a trait that had previously appeared to be an unredeemable fault. By finding the essential goodness in this trait, she gained hope as well as a strategy for personal growth. A more harmonious future stands before her now. From direct experience she learned this principle that is at the heart of Cayce's philosophy of good and evil: What appears to be evil is just under good, a seed of truth that's waiting to show its real essence.

EXERCISE

The aim of this exercise is to start redeeming one of your own personality traits, a characteristic that you recognize and usually label as a fault. By looking for the essence of good that resides within bad, you *won't* be trying to condone or excuse a shortcoming. Instead, you'll be *transforming* a part of yourself

Honestly examine your own personality and choose one trait that you consider a weakness or a fault. Spend some time reflecting on how this fault may contain a seed of goodness.

Then speculate on how you may be distorting this originally good impulse so that it manifests itself as a weakness. Are you overdoing, misusing, or selfishly expressing it? Or is this essential strength being distorted by fear or self-doubt?

Carefully observe your own actions. Notice when you use this trait positively and when you use it negatively. There may already be times when the basic strength comes through clearly without getting twisted.

Finally, make a special effort to keep this original impulse pure and positive. When you catch yourself expressing the urge negatively, stop and change the pattern.

PART TWO

New Ways of Looking at Your Life

Personal Alchemy:
Sometimes a Weakness
Can Become a Strength

Ancient alchemists were intent on a fanciful, seemingly impossible task: turning lead into gold. They imagined that something as ordinary as lead could somehow be transformed into the most valuable of all metals. At face value it would appear that they failed miserably. But maybe their esoteric writings were really coded messages. Perhaps the wisest alchemists knew that the authentic work of transformation occurs in the human mind and spirit.

What is the "lead" of your inner nature, and what is the "gold"? Personal weaknesses are common and ordinary, the all-too-familiar and unvalued aspects of every human being. Personal strengths—talents, abilities, and skills—are precious treasures. Could it be that through some sort of alchemical magic these two elements are related? That's an idea found repeatedly in the counsel offered by Edgar Cayce to people who were trying to understand themselves. Sometimes a weakness can be miraculously converted into a strength and shortcoming can become an asset.

What are weaknesses? In some ways they may be *undeveloped sides* of yourself, parts of your human nature that haven't yet emerged in healthy, mature ways. Fear, reluctance, feelings of incompetence, and repeated failure: these may be considered forms of weakness. One person may have a fear of relating to strangers, for example, or a reluctance to take even the slightest risk. A different person may feel completely inept at logical thinking, and someone else may fail again and again to assert her own will, letting outside influences control her. These are sample weaknesses, aspects of people that haven't been fully developed.

Another type of weakness is based on the *misuse of resources and opportunities*. You might encounter this as a tendency to excess: eating too much, talking more than you need to, being overaggressive toward people, being overly sensitive. Forms of selfishness—jealousy, greed, intolerance—also characterize this type of weakness. These are your so-called faults, the foibles and shortcomings that are most likely to trouble your friends and family members.

We all have weaknesses. Dwelling unnecessarily on them makes us uncomfortable and probably doesn't do us much good. However, there are times in life when we get the extraordinary chance to experience weaknesses of one type or another in a whole new way. Through a kind of alchemical magic, something happens to turn events around, and what has always seemed like a weakness is suddenly transformed. It has become a strength!

Edgar Cayce as Alchemist

The few individuals fortunate enough to receive a reading from Edgar Cayce might have experienced that transformative moment when they first read the typed transcript of Cayce's advice. These people saw their personal weaknesses described in a new light. When he was at his best as a spiritual counselor, Cayce operated like a skillful alchemist. Ordinary, commonplace human failings were reframed as potential assets. According to Cayce, a weakness is only a strength that is being misapplied or used in a vain way.

David Kahn was a forty-five-year-old businessman given the opportunity to see one of his shortcomings in a radically different way. His reading from Cayce pinpointed a weakness well known to David's friends and associates: he frequently talked too much. But rather than feel guilty or condemn himself for this weakness, he was encouraged in the reading to look for special occasions when that trait might be transformed into a valuable resource. There were chances to use his gift to be persuasive and lead people to a better understanding of life.

Rather than remain an annoying chatterbox, David became a compelling spokesperson for Cayce's work. Over the years that followed he personally persuaded more people to request help from Cayce than anyone else did. What might have remained a personal weakness was altered alchemically into a strength that served hundreds of individuals.

Another example may be found in the advice given to a young college woman who contacted Cayce, asking for guidance in her personal and professional decisions. Cayce's reading described her as supersensitive and therefore inclined to quick mood changes. Even though most people saw this as a character weakness, Cayce recognized it as a stepping-stone to helpful influences in her life. In other words, her supersensitivity didn't have to remain an obstacle; the same sharpness of perception that was quick to notice slights or slurs could be used in an alternative way. Life would regularly present this young woman with opportunities to focus her sensitive nature on the creative, constructive, and positive occurrences around her.

Reframing Weaknesses in a New Light

A common theme links these two stories. In both cases weakness was transformed into strength by something more than sheer willpower. Life itself was an ally: the circumstances of daily living presented tailored opportunities to reframe a weakness into an asset. This sort of transformation—an alchemy of consciousness—is akin to the concept of "making a medicine out of the illness." In surprising ways, character traits or personal conditions that seem to block us can sometimes be transmuted into the very thing that can help us most. Our job (largely) is to stay alert to these special moments.

From early American history we are provided with another illustration of the unexpected way in which this process can unfold. This true story concerns Clark Davis, a resident in 1827 of Independence, Missouri, and one of twenty-five men who conducted the first, and perhaps most foolish, silver expedition to Colorado. One of his friends, James Cockrell, claimed to have found a silver mine in Colorado four years earlier while on a beaver-trapping venture. In the summer of 1827 Clark, his friend, and twenty-three other frontiersmen set off on horseback to make their fortunes. James Cockrell was appointed leader of the group.

Crossing the Great Plains in those times was dangerous. Each man took only his horse, a rifle and ammunition, scant bedding, and enough food for the first ten days. Hostile Indians would be a constant threat during the trip. Yet the group successfully made it through two hundred miles where food was scarce and found itself following the Arkansas River westward through buffalo country. So all the way to the base of the Rocky Mountains a steady supply of meat was available.

Once they were in the proper region, the leader of the expedition had considerable trouble finding the silver deposits. Clark and the other men grew restless because they had come a long way. With a mutiny starting to develop, James Cockrell announced that he had rediscovered the valuable mineral deposits. However, the men were disappointed by what they saw: dirty-looking rocks with occasional bright specks of metal in them. Not one of the men had ever seen silver ore, nor did they know the first thing about mining. They had been under the delusion that large chunks of pure silver could be easily chiseled out with tomahawks and that they could quickly extract enough to make themselves wealthy for life.

Despite their disappointment and frustration, each one collected some of the outstanding specimens available, packed them on their horses, and then set out for home. The return trip went smoothly until they reached a point on the Arkansas River where Dodge City, Kansas, now stands.

They camped that evening, ate a hearty supper of buffalo meat, and went to bed. Two men at a time guarded the horses for fear that hostile Indians would try to steal them. On that fateful night the Indians succeeded in sneaking into their camp, fired their guns, and let out war whoops that frightened the horses away. The frontiersmen saved themselves by taking up positions along the riverbank and holding their adversaries at bay with rifle fire. But when the sun rose the next morning, they knew they were in a dire situation. It was late autumn, and they were four hundred miles from the nearest town, with no food or horses.

As the men contemplated their circumstances, they realized that things were looking particularly dismal for Clark Davis, the man in the group who was most loved and respected. For Clark had one extraordinary weakness: he was obese, weighing over three hundred pounds, with a body of short stature. They talked among themselves privately, agreeing that Clark had little hope of making it home. At first they thought they would have to leave him behind on the prairie so he wouldn't slow them down. However, their affection for Clark was so strong that despite his critical shortcoming, they decided to keep him with them. The men took turns carrying his rifle and ammunition. Each day five of them would walk with Clark at his rate, taking three or four hours longer than the rest of the group to cover twenty-five miles. The first week was torturous for Clark. His feet blistered terribly, and his limbs became exceedingly raw and sore.

The first two hundred miles of the journey on foot was through buffalo country, and food was easily accessible. The final two hundred would be the real test, because their only food during that stretch would be the little buffalo meat they could carry with them. As they started into that desperate phase of the trip, a remarkable change came over Clark. His condition began to improve. He and his bodyguard party lagged less and less behind the main group during each day's march. As they moved deeper into the region, *Clark actually began to lead the group!* His weakness had been amazingly transformed into a strength.

When the party was still more than one hundred miles from home, Clark alone had sufficient strength to go on. One morning when all the men gave up hope and were unable to keep marching, Clark went out by himself with his rifle to hunt for game. He returned with two deer—enough food to sustain them all for the remainder of the trip home.

At the end of this remarkable expedition the men agreed on one point about their adventures. When the crisis had come four hundred miles from home, what had looked like the greatest weakness in their group—Clark's overweight condition—proved to be the greatest asset, something more valuable than all the gold or silver in the Rocky Mountains. But without their love for Clark and their deep sense of community, that alchemical transformation of Clark's shortcoming would not have been possible.

Strengths and Weaknesses in Temperament: The Four Personality Functions

In a more theoretical context, Jungian psychology provides another explanation of how a weakness can turn into a strength. Both Cayce and Jung felt that one of the best methods for self-understanding is the study of *temperament*. Each of us is predisposed to experience life in certain ways. There are common human patterns of temperament, distinct styles of processing information, of seeing and responding to life.

Jung often worked with his clients' strengths and weaknesses in a system that included four universal personality functions. What shapes your temperament (or anyone else's), according to Jung, is the relative emphasis of some of these factors compared with the others.

1. The first function is *thinking*—the capacity to evaluate life situations using objective, impersonal methods.
2. Next is *feeling*—an approach to evaluating that is the mirror opposite of thinking. This function appraises circumstances in a more subjective, emotional, personal way. You probably have a tendency to favor one of these two approaches to judging and evaluating life over the other.
3. The third function, *sensation*, perceives reality in terms of what is concretely here and now; it relies on the physical senses to tell you what is real.
4. Your *intuition* function, by contrast, is more imaginative and perceives the possibilities of what could happen in the future. (For Jung the term *intuition* meant something broader than just ESP.) Again, your personal temperament style probably leads you to emphasize one of these functions over the other. Thus, while one function becomes a strength, the other becomes a weakness.

Let's consider how this might work in terms of two sample individuals. Greg's temperament is feeling-intuition. In other words, he's likely to include in a list of personal strengths words like *sensitive, sympathetic, imaginative*, and *future-oriented*. He is the sort of person who walks into a room and immediately sees what could be done to make it more attractive or to use the space more efficiently. If there are people in the room, he's quick to feel a rapport with them.

In his list of personal weaknesses Greg is likely to include comments such as *poor at analysis, clumsy with mechanical tasks, impractical,* and *frequently loses track of time.* By what alchemical sleight of hand could these weaknesses be turned into strengths? How could the underused thinking and sensation functions be made assets for him? Jung's profound insight was based on the extraordinary value of novelty and creativity to the growth process.

It is commonly recognized that *habit blocks inner development.* We can get stuck in ruts with our strengths. In other words, what we're good at becomes so reliable that sometimes we never explore beyond the boundaries of what's familiar. Greg may be so skilled and comfortable with his feeling-intuitive way of relating to life that his growth stagnates.

The very ingredients that can stimulate a breakthrough are Greg's frequently ignored functions of thinking and sensation. He may be error-prone initially as he tries to evaluate life situations with his logical, objective thinking function. He may be awkward at first as he attempts to deal with the world in more concrete, practical terms. But it's worth the risk. Fresh, spontaneous experiences will come, unhindered by routine and habit, and they will spur his inner growth.

Jane's thinking-sensation type of temperament is different from Greg's. An inventory of her weaknesses reveals how infrequently she draws upon her feeling and intuition functions. Jane has trouble expressing her emotions, she's a slave to the clock, and she has difficulty letting herself be playful and imaginative.

Jane gets a lot of positive feedback and reward from her strengths; she's well paid for her pragmatic, punctual behavior. But she's also stymied in her development. Life is just a bit too comfortable, predictable, and efficient. Her strengths are being used in such habitual ways that she's gotten herself boxed in.

Ironically, her so-called weaknesses can make all the difference for her now. As with Greg, the aspects of herself that have been underused and not allowed to mature can become tremendously beneficial, a source of new ways to experience life and herself. They will be channels for renewed vitality and creativity. At first Jane will be forced to go against what's familiar and what other people expect of her; this will take courage. However, something magical will happen when she listens to her feelings more often, goes along with the flow of the day even if it means running late, and trusts her imagination.

Both Jane and Greg will find that their old strengths aren't invalidated by this process. On the contrary—as their former weaknesses become unexpected assets, those familiar strengths will also be freed to operate in fresh, unhabitual ways.

EXERCISE

After some honest self-study, make two lists. On one list describe your strengths; on the other, your weaknesses. Try to be especially objective, accepting, and noncritical when you itemize your weaknesses. Each list will probably have about half a dozen items.

This exercise of transforming a weakness is like the exercise for the previous chapter; however, in this case it involves the observation of unfolding life events. That is to say, often life situations give us special opportunities to see a so-called weakness in an entirely different light.

Then trust that life is your ally. Watch for situations that will provide you the opportunity to experience in a completely different way something you've labeled a weakness. Be alert for these special moments. Be willing to risk a little and discover the personal alchemy that transforms a shortcoming into a valuable resource.

Anger, Used Correctly, Serves a Good Purpose

In 1943 a thirty-nine-year-old homemaker from Berkeley, Virginia, came to Edgar Cayce and asked for a reading. She hoped that several questions would be answered, timeless riddles that were as troublesome to her then as they are to most people today:

Why do I suffer disappointments and frustrations?

How can I improve my relationships?

What is my true purpose in life?

In order to help her with these issues, Cayce began with a look at her personality. The reading, using astrological symbolism, first described the woman's character and mentioned that the influence of Mars was strong in her personality portrait. In other words, she had a tendency toward anger, what Cayce called "righteous wrath."

The reading went on to identify her ideals, noting certain experiences in previous lifetimes that had helped shape them. (The concept of reincarnation cropped up in most readings in which personal advice was requested.) The roots of this woman's angry temperament were traced to an incarnation during the Crusades. Living as a Frenchman named Richleuex in that lifetime, the soul had taken up arms with a high sense of purpose. But the Crusades had proved to be a deep disappointment. This soldier found that his ideals never had a chance.

Certain leaders had claimed allegiance to lofty motives and then acted hypocritically in the opposite way.

This realization brought much disappointment and discouragement to Richleuex. Seeing how the original purpose of the Crusades had been twisted and misapplied, he became extremely angry.

That anger was not left buried in the history of the Middle Ages: the emotional pattern continued to affect the soul. In fact, it was still alive in the heart of a Virginian mother during World War II. Hypocrisy or misplaced ideals created in her a "righteous wrath," a character trait that her reading actually encouraged, saying that she could get angry and yet still not sin. In other words, righteous anger is a virtue. Then Cayce concluded his chairvoyant analysis of this character trait by stating that a person who has no temper is very weak, but the individual who can't *control* his temper is much worse.

This conclusion has an unexpected twist. Certainly we would agree that people who can't control their temper need to heal that part of their emotional life. However, it may sound strange to contend that the lack of a temper is also a problem. In fact, there's a tendency in many spiritual traditions to consider anger a *barrier* to spiritual growth. Since inner peace is the objective, it's often assumed that a kind of placid complacency is the goal, an unflappable tranquillity that knows neither anger nor desire, only beatific bliss. But just how realistic is that assumption? Given human nature, is the suppression of anger an appropriate objective?

We all know what it's like to be angry. That emotion seems to be fully developed even in the youngest infant. Does our spiritual growth really depend on eliminating all anger from our personalities? Perhaps it's possible to find a proper place for anger and still create the kind of future we desire.

Consider the story of a farm wife who lived with her family in northeastern Nebraska. A very religious woman who wanted sincerely to live according to Christian ideals, she took to heart a sermon she listened to one Sunday on the virtue of suffering in silence. Silently she vowed to apply this virtue in her relationship to her family.

As often happens when one is choosing a spiritual discipline, this woman found opportunities to test her commitment almost immediately. That Monday her husband came in from working on the farm and tracked mud over her newly polished floor. She cleaned up after him without a comment. Later her children came home from school, grabbed the cookies she had baked, and scrambled to the television without saying "Thank you" or even "Hello." She endured this rudeness in silence also, straining to maintain her discipline. Similar opportunities piled up throughout the evening, but just before bedtime her kettle boiled over. After being cut off in midsentence by a request for some service, she threw down her knitting, stood up in the living room, glared at her family, and shouted, "Look, I've been suffering in silence all day, and no one's even noticed! And now I'm mad!"

This little domestic episode became a favorite family story for years afterward. Everyone profited from the experience. The husband and children learned something about courtesy and appreciation; the woman learned that anger is not an emotion that can be eliminated just by willpower. In her case, attempting to repress it simply increased its intensity. Anger is a force that must be dealt with. To understand how, let's first look more closely at the nature of this powerful emotion.

What Is Anger?

The Cayce material describes anger as one of the fundamental elements of the human temperament. In portraying the full range of human character traits, the readings make use of astrological symbolism. The planet Mercury, for example, symbolizes intellectual activity; Venus depicts the force of love and attraction; Mars, of course, represents qualities of assertiveness, intensity, and anger or wrath. Each planet is emblematic of an essential part of human character.

Spiritual growth can be understood in terms of what we do with these basic parts of ourselves. The objective is to harmonize and channel these qualities constructively, not to eliminate them. The goal is to have values, motives, and ideals that can harness the vital forces in these pieces of the human jigsaw puzzle. Every piece has its part to play.

Anger, then, is neither bad nor good; it just is. Like intellect or love, it's an aspect of the life force with which we all have to deal. Will anger become a stumbling block that impedes you? Or will it be a stepping-stone in your spiritual growth? The answer depends solely on you.

Cayce's reading for the homemaker from Berkeley, Virginia, was apt. In referring to her fiery nature, he said, "This is well." In other words, her righteous wrath had much to offer. But the reading quickly followed with a warning not to put anything before the divine purpose within herself. Thus anger can be a powerful tool, but if it gets in the way of your highest purpose—your spiritual ideal—it can become a monkey wrench.

The ancient Greeks recognized the significance of the potent, fiery side of human nature. The parallel between Cayce's notion of anger and that of the ancient Greeks was described by author and philosopher Jacob Needleman. Speaking at a conference on comparative spiritual philosophies, Needleman mentioned the Greek term *thumos*. The word was difficult to translate, he explained, but it referred to a kind of spiritedness (like a spirited horse) and essentially described the part of us that loves victory, struggle, and combat. Plato considered *thumos* a major quality in the warrior type or warrior class of people. If *thumos* is directed toward the gratification of selfish desires, it can be incredibly destructive. However, under the direction of the highest part of ourselves—what the Greeks called the *nous*—it becomes a powerful tool in our struggle to improve life both within us and around us.

When Is It Appropriate to Be Angry?

A ten-year-old boy found a wallet on his way home from the playground. In addition to a full set of identification, the wallet contained several dollars. As he examined his find, a well-known phrase rang in his head: "Finders keepers." Armed with this bit of justification, he took the money and threw the billfold away. Continuing home, he made a happy detour to the five-and-dime and squandered his treasure on a variety of toys. At home, he explained to his mother with innocent candor how he had come by his new trove of toys. "Finders keepers" was the law; he had simply obeyed it.

His mother's reaction shocked and surprised him. Her face looked like a summer storm rolling in from the west. Her voice sounded like claps of thunder. The boy realized with painful and sudden clarity that he had made a grave error.

Yet the story doesn't end here. Beyond the anger there was instruction. First, the boy immediately replaced the cash with his own hard-earned savings from his newspaper route. Then he and his mother trekked to the playground in a vain search for the discarded wallet. In a desperate attempt at restitution, the boy left his replacement money with a clerk at a nearby store with instructions to "give it to the man who lost his wallet if he should happen by."

The intensity of this incident never left that boy's memory. Even in his adult years it continued to shape his attitude toward others' property and possessions. In this case, his mother's anger was both justified and useful. It was generated out of love—both for her son and for an ethical standard. The anger was *applied* toward an important lesson that was very effectively taught. (It should also be noted that once the boy's attitudes and actions had been corrected and restitution had been made, the mother's anger evaporated.)

Unfortunately, not all anger emanates from such a noble place within us. Sometimes we become angry because we don't get what we want. Or we may get mad because our efforts are being thwarted. On other occasions we may lose our temper when we feel we're unappreciated. Usually these forms of anger are linked to a distorted image of ourselves, which may stem from a lack of proper self-esteem or occur because we believe we are more important than others.

How Can Anger Be Used Constructively?

If the energy generated through anger is applied in the direction of your highest ideals, it can achieve miracles. Leslie D. Weatherhead spent most of his life as Methodist minister. Throughout his career he became increasingly aware of the limitations and inadequacies of the Christian church. He saw how it had effectively created a self-imposed slavery to accumulated dogma. After he retired in 1960, he sat down to write a book, which opened with these words: "We hear much these days about angry young men and women. I am an angry old man, and I feel I must get the fire out of my bones, as John Wesley would say, before I die." He then proceeded to write *The Christian Agnostic*, an earthshaking book that has influenced thousands of people since its publication in 1965 and continues to do so to this day. His honest account of mature faith has worked miraculous changes in the lives of many spiritual seekers.

Of course, the miracles achieved through the creative use of anger may be far more personal. In the 1970s, a struggling actress living in Los Angeles finally got fed up with the frustration of her career and settled into a regular day job tending bar in a neighborhood Italian restaurant. For several months she was delighted with the security of the job—the regular hours and steady pay. She felt lucky to have a "port in the storm" and had no desire to reattempt the challenges of a career in show business.

Then one evening she found herself at an informal reunion dinner with many of her former classmates and friends. Inevitably the conversation came around to what each one had been doing. Although there was no obvious "one-upmanship" going on, the young actress soon felt her ears burning and her heart pounding. As she listened to each one at the table tell about this and that current project or endeavor, she became furious with herself for having been so idle in exercising her artistic talents.

Her agitation persisted over the next several days. The ancient Greeks would probably say that her *thumos* had been activated. Cayce might have said that her Mars was in ascendancy. Quite simply, she was angry. She had to *do* something, but what? She grappled with this question and eventually, in collaboration with her husband, devised a plan. With him directing, she created and performed a one-woman theatrical presentation for her church. It was very well received, and as a result she felt much better about herself. She didn't realize at the time, however, just what her initiative had set in motion.

Soon afterward, several of her theater friends expressed an interest in following up her project with another presentation that would include them. Upon the successful completion of this second production, even more followed. Soon her church found itself involved in an entirely new form of outreach and ministry: quality theater. The tradition continued for years, even after the young actress and her husband had moved away. This little miracle for the church community came into being only because the actress let her anger motivate her to do something creative.

Pointing Anger in the Right Direction

Remember the insight of contemporary philosopher Jacob Needleman? Anger, that combative, assertive side of ourselves, needs an appropriate *direction*. Anger, or *thumos*, is best used to correct our own weakness, foolishness, self-deception, attachment, and inattention. When the higher self begins to take charge and constructively channel our spirited, fiery side, the anger begins to accelerate our spiritual growth. The key can be stated simply: *Let anger motivate you to* do *something—to change things.* First, let it stimulate you to change conditions in yourself. Second, let its impulse energize you to improve the world around you and create a better future.

What happens if we fail to understand that key principle? If we don't use our anger in this creative, inner way, then we are very likely to direct it outward. This can be destructive not only to ourselves but to the fabric of society.

The period of Christian history known as the Crusades is perhaps one of the most graphic examples of the misapplication of humanity's spirited, combative nature. This was a time when the "warrior ideal" was at its peak. Much of the literature of the period glorified war and the virtues of the warrior. Our treasured legends of Camelot and King Arthur and his knights of the Round Table were being created during the time of the Crusades, when the highest calling was the holy war.

Yet even at that time there was a dawning awareness in the hearts and minds of some people that this warrior ethic was falling short of true Christian ideals. Troubadours and poets began to recognize the need to redirect this warrior energy inward, toward the refining of one's own character. This awareness finally materialized in the literature of the day as the legend of the quest for the Holy Grail. The grail itself symbolized the highest spiritual ideals.

The various renditions of this legend successfully turned the warrior ideal inside out. Those knights in the story who were the best at swaggering and boasting failed in their search for the grail. Those who succeeded did so after a series of arduous adventures that tested their inner character for patience, sincerity, and, most of all, compassion.

We are all part warrior. *Thumos,* Mars, anger—all are a part of each of us. We can't eradicate this trait, so what do we do with it? Anger is like any other force. It has the power to destroy and the power to create. The way we use anger and how well we control it determine whether we suffer from or profit by it.

EXERCISE

The focus of this exercise is on *directing constructively* the anger that is bound to come up periodically in the course of daily life challenges.

When you feel yourself getting angry with a situation, try something other than two counterproductive options: explosion and repression.

Instead, first *feel* that fiery energy, listen to and experience its potency. Then let it be a motivator. Allow it to stimulate you to make some changes, first in your *own* attitudes toward the situation and then in the situation itself.

Finally, *do* something about that situation, *not in* anger but *based on* the energy of that anger.

PRINCIPLE #10

The Good You See in Others Is Also in Yourself

On his last record album John Lennon sings a lullaby he'd written to his young son, Sean. In it, Lennon affirms that life is indeed getting better continually in all ways.

Lennon's message to his son was one of hope and reassurance. Yet as listeners of his music, we also receive the blessing of this affirmation. As he sings, we, too, can feel a renewed faith in ourselves and the hope that all the events of life are leading somehow to something better.

John Lennon may or may not be a hero to you personally, but one thing is certain: For millions of people he served as a symbol for what they might believe in and accomplish. That's what heroes and heroines do; they exemplify qualities that other people admire, people who then, in turn, can learn to nurture the same qualities in themselves.

This magic could be termed the *psychology of admiration.* Simply stated, it says, "The good you see in others is also in yourself." Role models, then, are extremely important, allowing us to catch glimpses of our own best selves. They stimulate our development and stretch us to a new standard. Even though some heroes and heroines may reveal themselves to have feet of clay, the virtues that we admire in them still belong to *us.* And when we feel those positive qualities stirring within us, we are getting a preview of our destiny.

Edgar Cayce's Role Models

At around the age of ten Edgar Cayce received his first Bible. With his family he regularly attended the Disciples of Christ church in Hopkinsville, Kentucky. As a boy, Edgar loved going to church on Sundays and listened eagerly to the adults talk about religion and the Bible. He overheard people mention how often they'd read the book from cover to cover. Armed with this inspiration, Cayce decided he would read his new Bible once for every year of his life.

Of course, the hitch was that at ten years old, he was already behind ten times! But he built a little lean-to shelter in a small meadow near his home and there began seriously to fulfill his chosen discipline. For the next three years he took advantage of every opportunity to read his Bible in the privacy of his shelter. Though he understood very little of it at first, he eventually came to know the stories by heart. The main characters became like personal friends as he read about them over and over again. Finally, at the age of thirteen, Edgar had succeeded in reading the Bible thirteen times. It was during that period, while reading in his lean-to shelter late one afternoon, that he had a mystical experience.

As he later told the story to his biographer, Thomas Sugrue, he was reading his Bible at sunset and realized that it was nearly time for supper. Suddenly, with his eyes still on the page, he became aware of a bright light over his head, which he assumed was from a lantern carried by his mother, who had come out to fetch him for the evening meal. However, as he looked up, he met with a great surprise. The light that had caught his eye was emanating from the figure of an unfamiliar woman. Glowing as she did, she did not seem to Edgar to be an ordinary woman at all. Indeed, behind both shoulders there seemed to be shaded areas that looked to him very much like the tips of wings. In short, Edgar concluded that he was being visited by an angel.

The apparition spoke to him, asking, "If you could have anything in the world you wanted, what would it be?" Without hesitation, the boy answered that he wanted to help other people, especially children, who were sick. The visitor then promised that he was about to be given a wonderful gift. If he used the gift wisely, his prayer would be answered.

This event was the prelude to Cayce's psychic awakening. Almost immediately thereafter he began to exhibit hints of the extraordinary psychic powers that would surface more fully eight years later. For example, he discovered that by sleeping on his schoolbooks he could absorb their contents with photographic recall.

With all the amazing events in this story, it's easy to overlook a crucial point. Through the visitor's question, Cayce was given a test. Why did he answer as he did? Why did he want to help other people and cure ailing children? According to Sugrue, Cayce was thinking of his heroes—his role models—the apostles. He had read their stories more than a dozen times. He knew them to be healers, both physically and spiritually. He answered the way he did because he wanted to be like them.

The people you admire are crucial characters in your life. You could probably list several in your personal history who inspire and motivate you in one way or another. Yet each one is special in his or her own way; each one touches you differently.

You may want to make a list of your models either in your mind or on a piece of paper. Perhaps you know some of the people directly, while others may be historic characters or public personalities. The individuals you list won't be perfect, but each will have some quality (or set of qualities) that impresses you deeply. For each name you record, also make note of the excellent features you recognize in that particular person.

Once your list is complete, take a moment to put aside the people themselves and study only the qualities and features you've listed. Now ask yourself: What are the characteristics that I admire most in others?

According to the psychology of admiration, those *same* qualities are present in yourself. If they weren't there—at least as a seed, as a potential—you wouldn't recognize and appreciate their presence. Your feeling of admiration is the stirring to life of those same features within you. But the news is even better than that. Not only do these fine qualities reside within your own soul, but this excellence you glimpse in the heroes and role models you admire is a preview of what you are growing into and becoming.

Teleology—Better and Better

The Cayce readings offer a formula for moving toward our destiny. We can begin to see results almost immediately and then, step by step, see the realization of our finest potential.

This simple procedure begins with the belief that things can and do get better. The scientific word for this concept— the conviction that life is evolving according to a plan and design—is *teleology*. A teleologist would say that the whole universe, and each one of us within that universe, is planned and shaped toward a purpose. Although not everyone believes this, overwhelming evidence exists all around us to support it.

A charming fable illustrates the teleologist's point of view. One day a nonbeliever began to argue with a holy man concerning religious belief. The antagonist insisted, "You believe many things that cannot be proved. For example, you insist that the world was created by a divine hand. Can you prove it?" The holy man said, "Of course, but first let me ask you a question. What are you wearing?" This irritated the skeptic, who replied angrily, "What kind of a fool are you? Anyone can see it is a suit!" The holy man continued, "Who made it?" "A tailor, of course," the unbeliever replied. "Can you prove it?" the quiet sage continued. This annoyed the skeptic even more. "You are indeed a fool if you do not know that suits are made by a tailor!" Gently the holy man checkmated his opponent: "And you, my friend, are equally foolish if you cannot see the divine hand at work in creation. Just as a house displays the hand of a builder and the garment that of a tailor, so the order and beauty of creation testify to the skill and wisdom of God."

Get to Know Yourself

Once you've accepted the premise that you—along with everything else—are "getting better and better," you're ready for the next step in fulfilling your destiny. Begin by examining yourself as objectively as possible. It's not easy sometimes to look in a mirror that reflects not only your physical appearance but also your inner life.

Unfortunately, the process of self-observation carries with it two potential dangers: seeing yourself as better than you really are and seeing yourself as worse than you really are. Self-observation doesn't mean self-*glorification* or self-*condemnation*. Impartial self-reflection means being honest with yourself and measuring your thoughts and actions against your spiritual standards. In order to learn objectivity, it's sometimes helpful to regard what others say about you. But this, too, requires some discernment on your part. Even as you listen to the advice or opinions of others, you need to evaluate the quality of the source, as illustrated playfully in this story of the dancing bear retold by William R. White in *Stories for Telling:*

A particular bear was quite proud of his ability to dance. One day he was working on a new step and decided to try it out for his friend the monkey. "How do you like it?" the bear asked eagerly after he'd finished. "It's very bad. You look awful," said the monkey, who himself was quite nimble and agile. The bear was indignant. "You're not very polite," he said. "Didn't you like that jump I made at the end?" The pig, who had been listening to this exchange, suddenly chimed in, "Hurray for you, Bear. You are a magnificent dancer. I have never seen better!" The bear thought a moment about the two responses to his dance. He finally said to himself, I think I'd better practice these steps a little more before performing them again. I was indignant when the monkey criticized me, but my dancing must really be bad if the pig liked it so much!

See the Christ in Yourself

Although it may sound audacious, Cayce's spiritual psychology encourages us to recognize our own Christlike qualities. The fact that we can admire the characteristics exhibited by Jesus (and other great spiritual teachers) indicates that we possess those same qualities ourselves. A young man came to Edgar Cayce in 1944 seeking advice on how to succeed in life. Cayce offered both advice and a promise, telling the man to analyze himself carefully and thoroughly in body, mind, and soul. This type of objective observation would yield a great discovery: the counterpart of the Christ.

This is not to say that we should ignore our shortcomings. We still have lots to work on and overcome. But the highest truth about ourselves is the best that is in us. Now, how can we *recognize* those glimpses of our best when they appear? What does it *mean* to be at our best? The clue is to notice certain signposts. Many of them are feelings, and it's difficult to state them adequately in words, but here are a few descriptions of how you might feel in those moments when you're at your best.

1. *A sense of wonder.* When you're at your best, your senses are wide open and you more easily touch the miracle and mystery that is life—even in its tragic and painful moments.
2. *Compassion.* You are *approaching* your best when you are sensitive to others' feelings: their joys and their sorrows. You *are* at your best when your sensitivity spurs you to definite action.
3. *Forgiving.* This is one of the most difficult and yet most profound indicators that you are in touch with your divine center. Forgiving others doesn't mean becoming a doormat, allowing others to run roughshod over you. Rather, it means releasing grudges and resentments that have crystallized around past injustices. All of nature demonstrates this virtue, but only human beings know how to hold a grudge.
4. *Humor.* Humans are also the only residents of this earth who know how to laugh. Seeing the funny side of any situation brings a mysterious power. You're able to rise above the difficulty in a certain way, and from that place you may find a new perspective on how to handle it creatively. A sense of humor is definitely a spiritual gift.
5. *Humility.* This Christlike quality doesn't mean hiding your light or denying your own strengths. It means remembering the true source of your strengths and talents. It's a feeling of quiet thankfulness for all that you are, all that you have, and all that you can do.

Pick Your Role Models Carefully

When Cayce had his sacred vision at the age of thirteen, his responses to it were largely conditioned by his heroes, the apostles. He saw in them qualities that he wanted in himself. Any unbiased study of his life will clearly document that he did possess those qualities. The apostles he came to know so intimately through his tireless study of the Bible were in fact symbols of his own best self.

We all do this—identify with people we admire and try to emulate them. Our earliest role models are usually parents or siblings, and the specific traits we recognize and value in them are usually the same qualities we feel resonating within ourselves. The good we see in others already belongs to us; otherwise we couldn't recognize it. Throughout the Cayce readings, there is one role model that is held up and honored far above any other: the life blueprint demonstrated by Jesus. His is referred to as the perfect pattern on which we all can model our lives. The person of Jesus presented in the New Testament can serve as a symbol of our destiny as well as a guide for our actions. Cayce's readings often articulated this notion. To put this statement into practice, Cayce's readings often counseled people to make decisions by asking themselves, ''What would Jesus do?''

It's important for you to admire other people, allowing them to motivate you toward higher standards. But it's also important to realize that those same admirable qualities have their counterparts within you. They may be just seeds, but they're there inside you, ready and willing to germinate. Most important of all, however, is to recognize and remember your own finest moments. For in those moments, you're getting a preview, a taste, of your true destiny.

EXERCISE

The psychology of admiration can best be summed up in these words: The good you see in others is also in yourself. Consciously practice this principle for a day.

First, take a few minutes to review the key figures in your life. Notice what you admire in them. You may even want to jot down notes about what you recognize.

Now take these insights and affirm that the same positive features live in you, some of them fully developed, some just beginning to awaken, and some still dormant.

Finally, without ignoring or trying to cover up your faults and shortcomings, *believe in your own excellence*. Try living a day with this feeling: You *at your best* are a preview of what you are destined to become.

PRINCIPLE #11

Every Crisis Is an Opportunity for a Breakthrough

In 1901, when Edgar Cayce was twenty-three, he developed a bizarre and seemingly incurable illness. He lost the use of his vocal cords and could talk only in a whisper. This may not seem like a particularly terrible ailment, but to a budding insurance salesman planning to support his family with his new career, this illness was definitely a crisis.

He went to every doctor in the area around his hometown of Hopkinsville, Kentucky. Not one of them could even determine what was wrong, let alone figure out how to cure him. Finally, in desperation, Cayce went to a hypnotist. Traveling through Hopkinsville was Hart-the-Laugh-Man, a show business hypnotist working the local vaudeville circuit. Slightly embarrassed at pursuing such an unorthodox remedy, Cayce made his way to the backstage area of Hopkinsville's playhouse and made an appointment with the stranger.

This bold move born of his desperate predicament was the first step on a journey that led to Cayce's first psychic reading, a hypnotically induced trance from which he diagnosed his own ailment. His laryngitis was quickly cured when he followed the remedies suggested in this reading. His health crisis became a breakthrough to his life's destiny.

Indeed, Cayce's entire life can be seen as a series of such critical breakthroughs. In 1923 Arthur Lammers came to Cayce not with the usual physical concerns but to ask for a psychic reading on his astrological horoscope. This reading yielded the first reference to reincarnation, which brought on a *new* crisis for Cayce—a crisis in confidence. Doubting the reliability of his psychic information, Cayce turned to his spiritual touchstone, the Bible. At the end of this critical period he broke through to a profoundly deeper vision of his faith and of the book that was its spiritual voice.

In 1931 Cayce faced one of the most desperate crises of his life: the loss of his treasured hospital and the unfriendly breakup of his entire research organization. Like King Arthur facing the disintegration of the Knights of the Round Table, Cayce wondered if his life held any meaning at all. Yet out of this torturous midlife crisis at age fifty-four, Cayce opened the most spiritual chapter of his psychic career. It was during this next phase of his life that Cayce produced readings giving detailed instructions about the path of inner development and about spiritual healing.

Thus, the patterns of his life illustrate this spiritual truth often mentioned in the readings: Crises and trials are opportunities for breakthroughs in personal and spiritual growth. Cayce is not alone in this perspective. Virtually all spiritual wisdom offers this teaching in one way or another. In the ancient language of China, the written character that represents *crisis* is a combination of two other words: *danger* and *opportunity*.

The Gift of Crisis

All religions and mythologies speak of the critical tests faced by great spiritual teachers before their final victory. The individual who became the Buddha faced a supreme crisis before he achieved enlightenment. As he sat underneath the Bodhi tree, he was visited by the great Mara, "Lord Desire" of illusion. This invidious entity first insisted that he abandon his foolish quest for enlightenment and start living up to his social obligations. Then it came to him surrounded by voluptuous female spirits named Lust, Restlessness, and Greed, tempting the future world savior with carnal desire. When that failed, the Mara approached him in the form of "Lord Death," along with a horrible army of demonic forms with multiple mouths, lolling tongues, and pointed teeth. In their hands they carried bows and arrows, darts, clubs, swords, even blazing mountains. But through all this, Gautama Sakyamuni remained still, unmoved by desire, fear, or the necessity of social commitments. Only after these tests were met and overcome did he become the Buddha—"the Enlightened One."

The Christian savior Jesus faced a similar encounter when he retreated to the wilderness, fasting for forty days after his baptism. His temptations concerned hunger, pride, and power. After undergoing this testing crisis, Jesus began his earthshaking ministry in earnest.

Although the trials in these accounts are different, they touch on the same truth. Not only is every crisis a possible breakthrough, but most breakthroughs are in fact preceded by a crisis of some kind.

Mythologist Joseph Campbell describes the cyclical pattern of crisis and breakthrough with the term *monomyth,* or the "mythological round." All of us tread the path of the monomyth in our heroic quest toward spiritual fulfillment. In this cycle we (as the heroine or hero) are called to a journey, an inner exploration. Along this adventure we encounter challenges as well as assistance. The challenges will test our courage, our compassion, and our faith. Ultimately we are brought to the supreme test, which, if met successfully, is followed by a profound transformation. As a result of this rebirth, we discover new abilities or insights that can benefit us and others as well. Then we proceed once again along the cycle of growth.

Because this pattern is so fundamental, its evidence is everywhere. You can probably point to several illustrations in your own life. Cayce's psychic readings offer countless examples of critical situations that ushered in breakthrough experiences. In 1914 Edgar's son, Hugh Lynn, accidentally ignited a box of photographic flash powder, which blew up in his face. The local physicians announced sadly that he would never see again. The young boy, who had previously felt embarrassed by his father's strange ability, declared that when asleep his dad was a "wonderful doctor," and pleaded for a reading. Bolstered by his son's confidence, Edgar quickly complied. The psychically recommended treatments proved effective, and after that crisis Hugh Lynn became a tireless supporter of his father's work.

In 1937 a man came to Cayce seeking relief from anemia and a leg fracture that refused to heal. In the reading the man asked a pertinent question: "What was the purpose of my accident?" It turned out that for years he had had a powerful interest in painting but had done very little about it. The reading suggested that the accident had offered him an opportunity to get in touch with his true mission in life. He was told of an earlier incarnation in which he had found tremendous joy as an early Christian despite the fact that he was lame. He was advised to paint scenes of the life of Jesus with his disciples and was told that his purpose in life was to use his painting to bring hope into the hearts of all people.

Since Cayce's death in 1945, thousands have discovered in his legacy opportunities for a personal breakthrough. Not surprisingly, these discoveries are often made in the midst of crises. A man from London tells of his extraordinary suffering from arthritis of the hips. He was in such chronic pain that he could barely climb stairs. After serendipitously coming upon the Cayce material in a local library, he started applying the treatments for arthritis that Cayce had prescribed years earlier for other people. The man had such success with the treatments that he became a devoted teacher of Cayce's principles. In overcoming his physical crisis, he found new opportunities for service and commitment.

Breakthroughs Come in All Forms

A crisis in one area of life can create a breakthrough in another. In his award-winning play *The Shadow Box*, Michael Cristofer allows three stories to unfold simultaneously. Each is about a terminally ill patient and the impact of the crisis on his or her relationships. No one is miraculously healed in the play, yet profound healings are achieved in the various relationships involving wives, lovers, and children. The play is one of victory and breakthrough even in the face of inevitable death.

A similar story is found in one of Cayce's case histories. In 1929 a dentist suffering from hyperacidity got a reading regarding his ulcerated stomach. The reading offered treatments along with explanations of the causes of the affliction. The man was an atheist, full of fear and anxiety. These negative emotions, called "mental strain" in the reading, had helped create the ulcers, and their cure would require changes in attitude.

Despite the treatments, the man did not improve. Further readings modified the therapy but insisted that the individual could get better if he had the desire and followed all the recommendations. Eventually the man died.

On the surface it would seem that no change had occurred, yet after the man's death his son wrote to Cayce with the family's observations. The son admitted that his father had no spiritual interests at the point when he first sought Cayce's assistance. But after his father returned home from psychic readings and treatments at the Cayce hospital, his attitudes were completed altered. He had told his family members that now he knew there was a God. The unquestionable evidence came from observing Cayce himself—a man giving his life to help others. Even though the father's physical body had not survived the illness, something in his spirit had been profoundly healed.

A Method of Transformation

All crises are potential births. The nature of that birth depends on the particular crisis and the character of the individual. Fear and doubt can stifle the process. On the other hand, facing one's crises in a positive attitude of expectancy can help the birthing process along. Following is a four-step plan for transforming a crisis into a breakthrough.

Step One: Accept your condition

A Kansas farmer who had managed to live through seventy-five years of ups and downs was asked by a young acquaintance how he had been able to maintain his cheerful outlook on life for so many years. The old farmer said, "That's simple. When you're in a bind, you just figure out the worst thing that could happen to you, accept it, and then go on from there."

Without realizing it, the farmer had lived by a principle that psychiatrist Carl Jung identified as the first requirement for healing any condition. Nothing, Jung said, can be changed unless it is first accepted. Until then, a condition remains unapproachable and ominous.

The same wisdom is found in an ancient fable. According to the story, a village was frozen in fear and mourning because it knew that a dragon was planning to devour every person in it. Everyone could see the dragon on a far-off mountain, looming as large as fear itself. They could hear its horrible roar louder than the crack of thunder. Now, a young stranger happened by and decided to confront the dragon, so off he went to climb the dreaded mountain. Curiously, however, the closer he got to the dragon, the smaller it appeared. When he finally reached the monster, it was no larger than a cat and its fearsome roar had diminished to something like purring. The stranger tucked the creature under his arm and returned to the village. Everyone was amazed at his story and marveled at the cute little dragon that they'd held in such dread. Eventually someone asked the dragon's name, whereupon—to everyone's amazement—the dragon itself spoke: "I am known and feared by many names throughout the world, but ultimately all know me as 'what might happen.'"

Acceptance doesn't mean giving up. This word, according to Jung, means something far more positive than "resignation." On the contrary, acceptance is the bravest of confrontations. It's looking your situation squarely in the eye and saying, "Okay, I see you, and I know you're real. Now I'm going to take some action."

Step Two: Take responsibility for your situation

Events happen to you that are clearly beyond your direct influence. A tornado may crash through your town and may even destroy your home. How can you possibly take responsibility for such a crisis? On a surface level you can't. However, if you deny any responsibility for what happens to you, you're likely to consider yourself a victim of random circumstances. This sort of "victim consciousness" won't lead to any kind of breakthrough.

The theory of reincarnation can be helpful in addressing this dilemma. When circumstances seem to mark you as an innocent victim, you can still affirm within yourself that something deep in your soul has purposefully attracted this experience to you.

The danger in this past-life perspective is getting sidetracked into the puzzling question, What awful thing did I do in a past life that made me deserve such a fate? Unfortunately, it may be impossible to come up with a reliable answer. The mysteries of our distant soul past are likely to remain clouded. What's more, that line of speculation focuses on events from the past rather than those of the here and now. The important question is, How can I grow now from this experience? Best understood, reincarnation may be accessed as a tool that allows us to accept the present moment, taking responsibility for all aspects of our lives.

Step Three: Identify the quality you need to deal with this situation

You've probably heard the expression "If this doesn't kill me, it will make me stronger." There's wisdom in that statement. But in dealing with a real-life crisis, it's helpful to be as specific as possible in identifying the exact strength that the difficulty evokes from within you. One crisis may call forth assertiveness; another, gentleness. One problem may demand that you become more self-sufficient; yet another could require that you learn to achieve a balance between giving and receiving.

When you face a serious problem, try to determine what exactly is being demanded of you. By recognizing the quality or trait you need in order to handle the crisis creatively, you begin to usher in the breakthrough. As you strive actively to develop that feature, you are no longer a victim of circumstance but a hero or heroine along a transformative journey.

Step Four: Stay hopeful

The very fact that we are capable of hope provides evidence of the existence of the soul. In 1934 a woman came to Cayce beset with problems in her home life. Her husband was being unfaithful, and she was considering a divorce. At the same time, she was also feeling estranged from her children, and in her reading she asked repeatedly why she had failed in so many areas of her life. Cayce insisted that she had not failed and that she *would not fail* unless she lost hope and stopped trying. The same Kansas farmer who was willing to accept the worst summarized his philosophy of success this way: "Prepare for the worst and hope for the best." Without hope, all three previous steps collapse. Hope is the quality that sees us through the crisis and directs us to the breakthrough.

The importance of hope is not always recognized in our world. This may be due to the popular notion of what a hero or heroine is supposed to be. Few of our hero models ever get confused. They face each challenge with the confidence of a John Wayne—unflappable and almost indestructible. To the superhero, hope is unnecessary; victory is just a few sure strides away. But life in the real world is a different matter. Confusion and even chaos may buffet us. Indeed, a crisis by its very nature can often include periods of confusion that are necessary as we reorganize our lives. Hope keeps us going when everything else dissolves into confusion.

The entire course of human life can be seen as a series of crises, starting with birth. Every change thereafter is also a kind of birth. Some are predictable and well documented: the challenges of adolescence, the trials of adulthood, the midlife dilemmas that force us to regroup and prepare for more productive later years. Other serious challenges may come unexpectedly, but all contain the same opportunities to refashion oneself. Even death is just another crisis through which we are born again into a new dimension of life.

In every crisis we encounter opportunities for new life, growth, and understanding. Sometimes these periods demand the very most of us. Occasionally we may feel there is no way out of a situation, that we are "caught between a rock and a hard place." But like the Israelites who found themselves pinned between the attacking Egyptian army and the crashing waves of the sea, we may be surprised to find that there *is* hope—a breakthrough to a new land.

EXERCISE

Take a close look at your life. It may be full of crises: some small-scale and likely to pass quickly, others more serious or long-term. Pick just one of them in order to evaluate how you are doing so far in using that crisis to make a constructive breakthrough.

When you've made your selection of one crisis, ask yourself these questions in sequence:

1. Have I brought a feeling of *acceptance* to my situation?
2. Have I taken responsibility for the situation?
3. What are the qualities I'll need to deal with this situation?
4. Am I hopeful?

Then invest special attention and effort in any step that you haven't been applying successfully.

Life Is a Pattern of Cycles

Sometimes life seems totally unpredictable. Unanticipated bills arrive just when you think you've gotten your finances in order. An unwelcome ailment starts nagging just when you believe you're back in shape. A close friendship goes sour when you least expect it. How is it possible to plan reliably for the future when unforeseen events keep occurring?

Maybe life isn't as disordered as it sometimes appears. If we learn to look carefully, we're likely to discover patterns that help shape and give meaning to our experiences. Of course, those patterns won't predict everything. It's impossible to anticipate every life situation—and who would want to remove *all* the surprises, anyway? Nevertheless, we're a step closer toward building a positive future if we understand the undercurrents that continue to guide us.

The Cayce readings most often referred to these patterns as *cycles*. Cycles are time periods as brief as ninety minutes (the average duration between dreams as we sleep) to an entire lifetime (the cycle of the soul as it reincarnates). These numerous cycles are universal, part of the way every human is programmed. The more we know about them and how they work, the more easily we can be sensitive to their influence and plan our lives accordingly.

A simple illustration is found in one of the most basic cycles: the "circadian rhythm" of each twenty-four-hour day. Your body is a sophisticated clock that winds through many changes in the course of a day. Alertness, energy levels, and creativity are just three of the many factors that follow fairly reliable peaks and valleys in a given twenty-four hours. Although the exact nature and time of those ups and downs may differ from person to person, the rhythmic patterns are distinct for each individual.

For example, you may have discovered that you are a "night person," at your best and most creative late in the evening and even well into the period when most other people are sleeping. Knowing that your inspiration and productivity flow best during this time, you can plan your life accordingly. It would be foolish and frustrating to do otherwise. To force yourself to write a difficult business report right after breakfast would probably result in something far inferior to what you could produce much later in the day. The point is to get "in sync" with your cycle.

Cycles and Circles

A common root word links *cycles* and *circles*, but are the two words synonymous? Some evidence suggests so. The seasonal cycle of nature appears always to return to the same point. Native peoples, who are more in touch with the rhythms of nature, are inclined to create calendars that take the form of a circle. The Cayce readings referred to nature on many occasions when making the point that life is replete with rhythms and cadence. Astronomical cycles also appear to be circular: the progression of the planets and the stars across the night sky and the monthly passage of the moon around the earth. Cycles also play a major role in astrology. For example, the so-called Saturn return occurs at approximately age twenty-nine (and later at about ages fifty-eight and eighty-seven) and coincides for many people with significant changes in their life situations.

However, a subtle difference exists between a circle and a cycle in human experience, a distinction that can be observed only over a wide span of time. What in the short run seems like a circle may indeed really be a spiral. In effect, a spiral is a circle that is going somewhere!

A spiral makes a 360-degree movement but adds to it a progression along another dimension. In fact, seen without the benefit of depth perception, a spiral can look like a circle; however, it's that extra dimension that implies growth and development. Things may seem the same, yet they're not. For example, nature has gone through millions and millions of seasonal cycles. Every spring is the same as the last one in many ways, yet very slowly, through the process of evolution, change is taking place. Springtime this year was not quite the same as the one fifty million years ago.

The difference between a circle and a cycle is also demonstrated by the cycle of the soul referred to as reincarnation. Every lifetime is the same in many ways: birth, childhood, adolescence, adulthood, old age, death. Yet despite these familiar, repeated transitions in a life span, there is growth and development from one incarnation to the next. This was Cayce's view of reincarnation. We come back to an equivalent point on the curve and face a challenge much like the one from a previous lifetime, but now there is a chance to meet that opportunity in a new way.

Often the cycle of the soul is experienced without full consciousness. We may encounter an experience that feels significant—maybe even with a touch of "déjà vu"—and unbeknown to us it is a return to something from our soul's memory.

This concept of past-present familiarity was exhibited in one of Edgar Cayce's own remarkable dreams, which occurred on October 6, 1925, shortly after Cayce and his family moved to Virginia Beach, Virginia. The dream itself was brief: He was on a train but somehow got left behind. When a reading was taken to interpret the dream, a remarkable cycle of Cayce's soul was described. Three hundred years earlier, *to the very day*, he had landed by ship at this location that eventually became Virginia Beach. He had been one of the colonists who had come to live in Jamestown. We can only imagine what it must have been like to come to the New World and then be "left stranded" as your ship returned without you to Europe. That same theme was being played out for Cayce in the twentieth century as he and his family tried to find a new life for themselves in Virginia Beach. The soul returned to a familiar location and a fresh challenge: a cycle of precisely three hundred years.

Cycles of the Physical Body

The Cayce readings encourage us to look for cyclical patterns in both personal and social situations. For example, the collective experience we call the world economy is influenced by cycles, something that a few modern investment advisers have sought to chart and predict. According to Cayce, one of the most significant patterns is an economic downturn every twenty-four to twenty-five years. But at the level of *personal health*, Cayce was most explicit. Since two-thirds of this clair-voyant's work concerned healing, it's not surprising that these physical readings contain the bulk of his information on cycles.

One pattern that was frequently mentioned covers a twenty-eight-day period. This time span closely matches the lunar cycle as well as the average time between menstrual periods. Many of Cayce's natural treatments—for women *and* men—were suggested for a four-week duration, indicating that the body's elimination systems operate on such a cycle. On other occasions Cayce referred to much shorter cycles, even the circadian rhythm of twenty-four hours. For example, he in-dicated an innate tendency for greater blood circulation and muscular activity in the upper body limbs during the day and for the trunk and lower body during the evening. This corre-sponds with his recommendations for calisthenic or stretching exercises: upper body in the morning, lower body in the eve-ning.

Another approach to cycles relates to the application of health remedies. Cayce's healing philosophy often included suggestions for on/off sequences of treatment. Certain reme-dies, such as castor oil packs and Atomidine (an iodine-rich fluid taken a few drops at a time), were to be used for several days in succession and then stopped for several days. Presum-ably the days of nontreatment allowed the body to consolidate the effects of the remedy and then respond out of its own resources. Vitamin supplements (if one's diet was insufficient) were also recommended with this kind of on/off cycle so as not to make the body overly dependent.

Without doubt the most significant physical cycle described by Cayce is the seven-year period of regeneration. It is under-stood that every cell of the body is rebuilt within this time span. Many people find this claim to be both encouraging and disheartening. That *any* condition can potentially be trans-formed is reassuring; the discouraging news is that it may take years and years to see results.

In an age of wonder drugs and miraclelike surgery, we aren't inclined to wait seven years. We want healing *now*, and we've been led to believe that some pill or injection can solve almost any physical ailment. The voice of a nontraditional "clairvoyant physician" can barely be heard above the roar of an impatient technological society that tends to treat the body like a machine. Nevertheless, some conditions in our bodies cannot be rushed or changed overnight, and one of them is the innate cycle of seven years.

Of course, this isn't to say that relief from pain takes seven years. Both modern medicine *and* Cayce's natural remedies can produce relief for many illnesses in a much shorter period of time. The key idea, however, is that the re-creation of total health—not just the removal of uncomfortable symptoms—is a slow process and requires patient, persistent effort.

Think for a moment about your own body. Consider the possibility that you are not the same person physically you were seven years ago. There may be obvious signs of change, such as a weight difference or more gray hair, but Cayce meant something more basic. Your heart cells are not the same; you have different blood cells, new skin cells—a body that has been *entirely* replaced! But is it really much different? In the natural cycle of regenerating your body, you may have *re-created* many weaknesses and illnesses. That's what happens to most people.

But it doesn't have to be this way. Over the coming seven years you may be able to transform every point of weakness, shortcoming, or disease in your body. Cayce made the claim bluntly in one reading: A mind that feeds purely on spiritual things for seven years will produce a body that is a light to the world, but a mind that feeds solely on material, selfish things can produce a body like Frankenstein's monster. Of course, there are points in between these two extremes, but the future of your body is up to you: it's within your power during the coming seven-year cycle to create total health.

Psycho-Spiritual Cycles

Indications in the Cayce material point to regular cycles of development that pertain to the *mind and soul* as well as to the body. For example, a twenty-seven-year-old civil engineer wrote to Cayce requesting a reading. Earlier that year his mother had received assistance from Cayce, and he thought that this unusual source of information might be equally helpful to him.

In presenting a clairvoyant view of the man's soul's experience in this lifetime, the reading encouraged him to look for cycles of psychological change. It suggested that he look back and notice what had happened in seven-year increments: intense periods in which new forces came into his life. Cayce indicated that spiritually oriented desires and creative drives had been particularly influential on his conscious mind at the ages of seven, fourteen, and twenty-one. Then the reading predicted that age twenty-eight would be the start of a new cycle with similar effects. But the impact wouldn't be felt on his birthday alone; it would spread out over a fourteen-month span, beginning two months before his twenty-eighth birthday and lasting the entire year in which he was twenty-eight. There is little in the follow-up correspondence between Cayce and the young man's family to let us know how accurate this proved to be. Sadly, however, there is a brief note that he died tragically close to his thirty-fifth birthday.

We can find considerably more details about psycho-spiritual cycles by looking at the work of Rudolf Steiner. From among the many esoteric systems of thought, the ideas of this social philosopher are arguably the closest to Cayce's. Steiner, too, believed that seven years is the duration of the most influential cycle in a human life span. However, rather than focus on bodily changes, he emphasized the inner development that takes place during each of these periods, distinct phases marked by transition points at ages seven, fourteen, twenty-one, twenty-eight, thirty-five, and so on.

To illustrate, during the first seven years of life, the *soul* of a child continues the process of incarnation. The spiritual world is still more or less accessible. If this psychic umbilical cord is cut prematurely, it has detrimental effects on personality development, an impact that may not be observed until much later in life. For this reason, Steiner felt that before the age of seven (represented bodily by the new cycle that comes with the emergence of permanent teeth) concentrated intellectual pursuits should be avoided. Mental activities that force a child to develop logic or rote memory, such as arithmetic and reading, should be reserved for later, and in their place we should offer a young child artistic and imaginative activities.

Steiner developed an extensive curriculum of childhood education based on this notion of seven-year cycles: the Waldorf School movement (named after the place where the first school began shortly after World War I). In the grade school years between the ages of seven and fourteen, a soul is now ready for new phases of learning, including reading, writing, foreign languages, and arts and crafts. However, more abstract thinking should be reserved for the third seven-year cycle, which commences with puberty.

Of more interest to most adults is the extension of this theory into the years following age twenty-one. The first adult cycle is focused largely on pursuits related to social and vocational decisions: picking a marriage partner, starting a family, selecting an occupation. These challenges are more than simply social imperatives, according to Steiner. During this seven-year cycle innate psychological and spiritual development makes these issues particularly relevant. In the next cycle (ages twenty-eight to thirty-five) a certain independence of thinking begins to emerge. The individual has the opportunity to develop autonomy of belief and conviction. In Steiner's theory this maturation leads to a great turning point: age thirty-five and the start of the sixth cycle.

The period between ages thirty-five and forty-two is well documented as a stormy one. The midlife crisis sets in. A high percentage of marriages founder. Careers no longer seem meaningful. Although few people begin their midlife crises at age thirty-five, Steiner suggested that something very significant occurs in this seven-year period. Until this age a certain innate psychological development will proceed (unless blocked by unusual circumstances). A natural flow of maturation takes one as far as age thirty-five but then no farther. From that year onward, our success or failure rests largely with our own efforts and the use of free will. Each new seven-year cycle will have challenges. Some people will begin to feel like they are going around in circles, usually the ones who aren't making responsible use of their free will. But other people—the ones who creatively seize the opportunities in living—will experience each new cycle as a spiral of growth and unfolding.

Recognizing the Big and Little Cycles All around Us

Of course, not every meaningful cycle is locked in to a seven-year format. Alongside the more lengthy and universal patterns of which Cayce and Steiner spoke, we can also find shorter, more personal patterns. For example, by carefully reviewing your own history, you may discover that you've moved every four years or that you've made a job change every five. Or you may find that every six months you face a health challenge and every two years feel a deep need for a spiritual retreat.

Don't expect everything to change with each new cycle. Sometimes, as you begin a new period, many situations and key characters in your life will stay the same. But even in transitions that offer some stability, you're likely to find that old friends and acquaintances begin to play new roles *and* that new people come into your life to fill old roles. A mentor may become more of a colleague, making room for a new teacher or role model. Your closest, most intimate friend may become an infrequent companion, making room for a new best friend.

But what can you *do* with this idea of cycles? If you're convinced that life is sometimes shaped by these invisible patterns, how does this knowledge help you live in today's world? How can an understanding of the cyclical nature of life help you create a better future for yourself? Here are three practical ways to make use of this idea:

1. *Adopt a new attitude toward your body*. The typical point of view as one grows older is to see the body as a slowly deteriorating machine. Instead, consider that every seven years your body is rebuilding itself. What kind of body do you want seven years from now? Keep in mind that you can do something about making that ideal picture a reality. It will take persistence, but the fundamental cycle of physical regeneration makes it possible.
2. *Look for right timing when you take an initiative*. One sign of wisdom is knowing when to act and when to wait, being sensitive to the right moment for speaking and the best time for listening. The idea of cycles suggests that proper timing is a key to optimal results.

   Although most of our attention is usually directed to the beginning or end of a cycle, every point in the process is significant. Imagine, for example, that a woman observes a four-year cycle in her own vocational experience. Every four years she has either gotten a promotion or switched to a new company. The key to understanding and working creatively with such a pattern lies in recognizing the many intermediate points in that time span and taking advantage of the situations and opportunities that may repeat themselves; it isn't just a matter of waiting for the next four-year transition point to roll around. Maybe this woman will realize that at the two-year mark she usually has some professional failure that creates a crisis in confidence for her and her employer. Or perhaps she'll recognize that at the three-year point one of her new ideas results in an impressive success, setting in motion new possibilities that will eventually blossom in the following four-year cycle.

Within a cycle—whether it's related to your vocation, health, relationships, or spiritual life—there are optimal times for any initiative. As you become more aware of the many cycles that exist simultaneously in your life, you'll be better able to make choices. When you face a decision, ask yourself, "From looking back at my life, can I see how this current situation is part of a repeating pattern? Right now, where am I in that cycle, and what sort of effort is most likely to work best?"

3. *Recognize new opportunities within old challenges*. Nothing is more frustrating than reencountering a problem you thought you had already solved. The principle of cycles shows how the recurrence isn't due to past failure; if you are on a spiral of growth, you can expect familiar situations to come back. However, with each one you can lift the quality of your response to an even higher level. Try holding the mental picture of a spiral when you encounter one of these recurrent problems. Imagine that your personal growth is traveling along that ascending loop and that you now have come back to a familiar point. Hold clearly in mind that now you are one notch higher: you can meet this accustomed difficulty with more mature and loving reactions.

Cycles are a reminder that the universe is orderly. In a world that so often seems chaotic, they demonstrate a natural rhythm to life. Whether we are conscious of them or not, they shape our experiences every day, every year, and even every lifetime. Our challenge is to recognize these fundamental patterns of living and, by working in sync with them, create a better future for ourselves.

EXERCISE

Take about one hour of uninterrupted time to review your own biography. Make notes about key events in your past by writing them down on a timeline you've drawn on blank paper. You may find that this exercise will work best if you have several timelines, one each for your history of (1) personal health and sickness, (2) vocational interests and accomplishments, (3) love relationships, (4) other relationships (friends *and* enemies), and (5) spiritual growth. If other themes seem equally relevant, make timelines for them, too (for example, money, moving your residence). Make notes about the highlights you can remember.

Once you've finished your timelines, look for patterns. Although seven-year cycles may be fundamental for human experience, you're likely to see personal cycles of a different duration, too. For example, you may find a three-year cycle related to illness or recognize a five-year cycle in which another significant close friend comes into your life.

Finally, use your timelines to look into your future. What situations might you expect if some of those cycles continue? How can you best prepare to meet those challenges, both the difficulties and the exciting opportunities?

PRINCIPLE #13

Everything Happens for a Reason: You Have a Purpose in Life

What type of person came or wrote to Edgar Cayce for a reading? Most were uncomfortable with or suffering from a difficult life situation. A great many had physical ailments, but the second largest group had a discomfort within the soul. They requested "life readings"—psychic discourses about the meaning of life.

This particular type of reading from Edgar Cayce has gained renown over the years because of the fascinating past-life tales. Each of the nearly two thousand readings in this category contains from three to six brief stories that helped individuals gain insights about their talents and difficulties. It was not Cayce's intention to entertain people with clairvoyant visions of the past, however. The most important purpose of the readings was to help individuals understand the purpose of life and find the particular calling for which they were born.

Often we forget how valuable this kind of understanding can be. It's obvious that we need help when we have a serious ailment such as heart disease or even a temporary upset of the body such as indigestion. The pain and discomfort are clearly focused and can usually be pinpointed in a specific organ. Sometimes it's not so obvious that the wounds of the soul also require relief. Those needs are easily masked, and the pain is often difficult to identify.

The most frequent discomfort of the soul comes from lack of meaning. Just as the physical body must have air, food, and water, the human soul requires meaning. This point is emphasized not only in the Cayce material but also in modern psychology. Viktor Frankl, author of *Man's Search for Meaning,* among other works, was the founder of logotherapy. While an inmate in Nazi concentration camps during World War II, Frankl found that the prisoners who had a reason for living were the ones who were able to withstand the most horrible conditions imaginable. For many of those prisoners, that reason for living was linked to their vocations or their human relationships.

Both Frankl and Cayce felt that the spiritual element within is the key to meaning. For example, Cayce's readings encouraged people to find a purpose in life bigger than themselves and then to work responsibly toward it. Frankl counseled his clients in the same manner in the years after his concentration camp experience. We should stop asking what we expect *from life,* he counseled, and instead ask what life expects *from us.*

What *does* life expect from me? What is the meaning of my life? Where is the meaning *in* my life? The answers to these questions are extraordinarily hopeful. Every life counts, and each person has a valuable role to play. But life expects you to fulfill the mission for which you were born. Cayce indicated that each soul comes into the earth experience with such a mission, that we all have a significant contribution to make in the world. Frankl clearly stated his belief that everyone has a specific vocation, an assignment that demands fulfillment. Within your reach is a specific purpose, and you are well equipped with the necessary talents to carry out that purpose.

Everything Happens for a Reason

In a world that seems full of random events and general chaos, how can anyone find his or her way through the labyrinth and achieve a spiritual mission? Isn't it merely a matter of luck? Success appears to depend on unpredictable good breaks. But even though events may look disordered and confused, hidden forces do guide our life experiences.

While giving a lecture about the inner workings of reincarnation and karma, Rudolf Steiner invited his audience to try the following thought exercise. The exercise was designed to help us get in touch with the meaning behind any event, especially the challenging problems that sometimes seem completely purposeless, the ones that leave us thinking or asking plaintively, "*Why* is this happening to me?"

To complete this thought exercise, you'll need to select a recent personal misfortune. Once you've made your selection, imagine that another self lives in you, one that is far wiser than your ordinary self. This higher self is capable of constructing life situations and then leading your ordinary, conscious self into them. It is also able to design circumstances that have a purpose and a lesson to them.

In your imagination try to *be* that higher self. Think back to the particular event that your ordinary self has labeled a misfortune. Remember why you created this set of circumstances. What was the opportunity for learning and growth that you had in mind when you created this situation?

Sometimes this thought exercise isn't easy. Ordinary consciousness can be very resistant, putting forth arguments that may be tough to overcome, for example, "I'm not to blame for this misfortune because someone else was doing it *to me*." Or its rationalization might be, "My higher self would never play such a trick on me!" Yet Steiner indicated that we should persist in this exercise. In fact, life conditions *do* happen for a purpose, and even though we must sometimes suffer, there is a deeper meaning to be found in even the most troublesome events. Cayce echoed this principle as he instructed people to recognize that life is purposeful. Everything happens for a reason.

Personality versus Individuality

Steiner's thought exercise requires us to envision a hidden self that often has an agenda quite different from that of our ordinary self. In the language of the Cayce readings, these two aspects of self are called the *personality* and the *individuality*. This distinction is probably the most important concept in Cayce's psychological system.

The personality (or the ordinary self) is the one with which you are most familiar—made up of your likes and dislikes, beliefs and biases. But the personality is not only your inner life of attitudes and emotions; it's also the way you appear to others—your facade. In fact, Cayce's use of the term *person-*

ality closely resembles Jung's expression *persona*.

The personality functions largely by habit, with routine ways of thinking, feeling, acting, and reacting to the world. It's a necessary ingredient for living in the material world, since some activities (such as driving a car and eating) can be performed effectively without full conscious attention.

But where did the personality come from? For the most part, this ordinary self is the product of imitation. From earliest childhood we learn patterns from parents, teachers, books, radio, and television. This inclination to copy others is strongest in childhood, as any parent has no doubt observed, but continues in adult life as well.

The problem arises when this ordinary self tries to assert too much authority, when (1) your habit patterns begin to control everything and (2) you start to identify yourself fully with the personality and forget the individuality.

The individuality is the real self in the sense that it is permanent and continues from one lifetime to another. It is capable of authentic creativity and free choice, while the personality self is rooted in habit and rarely exercises the will. The mission that the soul has selected for a lifetime resides within the individuality. It is from this aspect of yourself that you gain *knowledge of* your mission and access the resources required for its *accomplishment*.

Certainly the personality has a role to play as you fulfill your soul's purpose. However, its job is to be responsive to the direction of the individuality. The ordinary self can become the vehicle of expression for the higher self. For example, your personality has developed certain skills and abilities over the years. But talents don't create a meaningful life by themselves; they can fall into nonproductive ruts or be directed by selfish motives. You begin to fulfill your soul's mission when the individuality starts guiding those abilities so that they are fully creative and used for service in the world.

Finding Your Purpose

How can you go about finding the exact nature of your soul's purpose? Several hundred people were fortunate enough to receive precise guidance from Cayce in their life readings. But if you don't know a gifted clairvoyant who can assist you, what steps can you follow?

First, believe in yourself and in life. Make a conscious effort to trust that life is purposeful and that events happen for a reason. Cayce even suggested that *every day* something happens that provides you with an opportunity to get more fully back on track with your mission. It's a sad fact that most of us ignore or misunderstand many of those situations. We misinterpret them as annoyances or inconveniences simply because the familiar personality self wants to stay in control. It recognizes those moments as a challenge to its authority and habit patterns.

Belief in yourself also means acceptance of your own greatness. You and everyone else you meet are extraordinary. This may sound illogical. How can *everyone* be extraordinary? We usually think the word implies an elite category of people who stand out from the crowd. But isn't every snowflake with its unique, intricate pattern extraordinary? Wouldn't every sunset or lightning storm qualify, too? Human souls are the same way. Each one is a wonderful, unique blend of talents and sensitivities. Every soul is equipped to make remarkable contributions to the community and world in which it lives.

Yet many of us fear our own greatness. This tendency was first articulated by Abraham Maslow, one of the founders of humanistic psychology. Maslow felt that even though we all have an impulse to improve our lives, many people attempt to avoid this aspect of their development. In *The Farther Reaches of Human Nature,* he called this the Jonah complex, after the biblical Jonah, who tried to reject the prophetic calling that God expected of him. This evasion of one's destiny or potential is, as Maslow put it, the fear "to become that which we can glimpse in our most perfect moments."

When you muster the courage to believe in yourself and in life, the next steps to finding your soul's purpose are straightforward, following the sequence that formed the outline of most of Edgar Cayce's life readings. Cayce worked with those who received his readings, helping them answer the four questions below, but you can find the answers for yourself with some careful, honest self-examination.

1. *What is your spiritual ideal?* In your peak spiritual moments, what have you recognized to be the highest truth about yourself and about life? On those rare occasions when the problems, demands, and busy agenda of your personality have briefly disappeared, what feelings awakened within you? The peak experiences were a glimpse at life through the eyes of your individuality self. What you can later recall of those moments can fittingly be called your spiritual ideal. This ideal is not strictly your "mission" in life but, rather, describes a place within yourself—a state of consciousness—from which that mission may be directed. Here, for example are words or phrases chosen by four different people as each one tried to clarify his or her spiritual ideal: joyful surrender, freedom, peaceful creativity, and oneness without fear.

2. *What are your key talents and abilities?* Cayce masterfully surveyed the assets and resources of individuals as he gave a life reading. Unfortunately, he's not available to you today. Nevertheless, by taking a quick inventory of your aptitudes and past successes, you can probably come up with a list that is perfectly adequate for this step.

   As you itemize, be sure to include talents that you sense are within you even though you may not have had much of a chance to use them yet. Call to mind abilities that you already apply on a regular basis, even though some may have gotten stuck in noncreative ruts and aren't being used to further your real purpose. Look for skills dealing with people, objects, and information—the three classic areas in which personal strengths reside. Think back to your most significant accomplishments and recognize the abilities that were required. You'll probably find that you can compile a list of six to ten of your most noteworthy talents and skills.

3. *What words capture the essence of your mission?* A short, thematic summary of your soul's purpose helps you implement what you were born to do. What's needed is something more specific than "To be loving" or "To serve God," since we all share these aspirations. Your mission statement should more precisely fit your talents and the contribution you are here to make.

That mission theme, which is usually expressed in four to fifteen words, describes how you will use your talents and what kind of creative service you will offer. However, it's not merely a job definition such as carpenter, lawyer, or secretary. Your mission may or may not be fulfilled through the occupation by which you earn your living. It's a great joy when that's possible, but there may well be times in your life when your mission is fulfilled most directly through your free-time activities and so-called hobbies.

Take a look at the following four mission statements. The first two are from the Cayce readings; the other two are from people who have discovered their soul's purpose on their own.

- To help people through transitions in their lives
- To edit and reshape the ideas of others so those ideas can be better understood
- To be a spokesperson for peace
- To be a stimulus for new ideas in the world

4. *How will you put your mission statement into action?* It's not good enough merely to know what your purpose is. Application is necessary. However, it is well to begin with little steps. Formulate a plan that involves two or three practical initiatives that will test the accuracy of your mission statement. Until you actually give expression to your statement, you won't know for sure if you have correctly identified your mission.

Of course, you can hardly expect every small experiment to be a rousing success. But some of them should bear recognizable fruits if in fact you've properly discerned your calling. Look for some or all of the following as encouraging signs:
- Greater joy
- Events falling into place or your being at the right place at the right time
- Seeing benefits come to other people
- Feeling closer to God
- Recognizing how all of life is purposeful

- Experiencing reserves of energy that seem to come from beyond yourself

Is Overcoming Karma Your Purpose in Life?

Although we've focused so far on the creative mission that allows us to contribute to the world, two other aspects of purpose in life should be mentioned. First is the development of talents for future incarnations. The theory of reincarnation usually makes us look backward in time, curious about who and what we have been. But the theory also invites us to look ahead: we'll be here again. Right now we are nurturing seeds that will sprout and grow in future lifetimes. One purpose in life is to start work now on the development of skills and abilities that will be integral to missions in future incarnations. We can practice what might be called preincarnation, the conscious preparation for later lifetimes.

Another aspect of one's purpose in life is overcoming negative karma from the past. We all incarnate with patterns of selfishness and misunderstanding that need to be healed. This work is distinct from the mission that contributes creatively to the world, but the healing of karmic patterns may sometimes be necessary before much progress can be achieved with the mission.

This point is illustrated in a life reading for an eleven-year-old boy who was a frequent bed wetter. Cayce gave medical advice to the parents that was designed to help with this difficulty, but then he proceeded to describe the problem from a spiritual perspective. Details of a past were offered, one in which the boy's soul had been incarnated as a pastor during the New England witch trial days. He had taken it upon himself to identify children who were hearing voices (authentically from spirit beings, Cayce suggested) and saw to it that those youngsters were ducked in a local pond to cleanse them of evil influences. Apparently this was traumatic and painful to the children, and this soul carried with it the guilt of such self-righteous behavior. In the current lifetime, now as an eleven-year-old, the soul was ducking itself symbolically by wetting the bed at night, a kind of self-imposed punishment.

Cayce went on to describe two other lifetimes that had been more positive. In ancient Greece the soul had made major accomplishments in several art forms. In Old Testament times he had been a friend of Joshua and had learned the gift of spiritual leadership. Cayce continued the reading and identified precisely the mission for which this soul had now incarnated: to be a spiritual leader, using the arts as a means of expression.

However, both the boy and his parents were warned in the reading about the possible effect of negative karma from the witch trial days. Unless the bed-wetting problem was overcome before the boy was fourteen, he would probably develop a very poor self-image and never claim those positive talents for his adult life. Unfortunately, there is no follow-up correspondence in the Cayce files from the boy or his parents, so we don't know what happened.

Nevertheless, this case, like many others, illustrates an important theme in Cayce's philosophy about the purposes for which we incarnate: we are all here for important reasons. There are aims related to the needs of other people. There are objectives focused on lifetimes yet to come. And there are intentions with the soul to correct mistakes and misdeeds from the past. With all this going on at once, no wonder our lives seem so full and busy!

EXERCISE

There are two fundamental ways of viewing your life: from the perspective of your personality self and from the angle of your individuality self. It's from this second point of view that you're most likely to see the purposefulness of even the most disturbing life situations.

Practice the "thought exercise" that asks you to shift your perspective from your personality to your individuality. At the end of the day, look back and pick one situation that upset you, something that might have appeared senseless and without purpose.

Then imagine that another self lives in you that is wiser and more fully in touch with your needs for growth. Try to increase your awareness and become that self for a moment. When you feel that you've momentarily shed your personality and become your individuality, ask yourself these questions: For what purpose did I create that difficult situation? What was the purpose for its occurrence, even though it may not have been evident to my personality self? Let the answers that come help you understand the opportunity that exists in that difficulty.

PART THREE

Free Will, Destiny, and Relationships

God Wants Us to Learn How to Make Decisions

Decisions, decisions. Some days the number of choices we face is almost overwhelming. As consumers we have an amazingly diverse array of options: dozens of different breakfast cereals, automobile models, and clothing styles. For entertainment and relaxation there are dozens of cable television stations, nearly countless movies at the video rental store, and myriad vacation alternatives.

But the decisions we need to make aren't found only in the outer world; in our inner lives we also have the opportunity to make choices every day. We can select attitudes to hold in mind toward life situations, and we can also pick our feelings and motives.

Some people long for a less complicated life, a world in which they still have their freedom, but without so many options. To them it seems as if spirituality might come more easily if so much time and attention weren't wasted on all the daily decisions. They may even find themselves looking for a new life-style to simplify matters.

For other people the problem is an anxiety that perhaps the right decisions are not being made. They wish for certainty, for signs from God that point one way or the other. These individuals sincerely want to follow a life path that is spiritually attuned, but sometimes they don't see clearly which choices will lead in that direction.

What Is the Will?

The key to the question of decision making is the human will. What is this mysterious ingredient that allows us to make independent choices? Those who believe that our lives are basically preconditioned claim that learning and habit patterns predetermine what happens to us. Others have recognized the existence of free will but describe it in a limited way: willpower that operates by grit and entails the suppression of desires.

The psychology found in the Cayce readings offers a different point of view, one that deeply appreciates human volition. The will is presented as one of the three attributes of the soul, along with mind and spiritual energy. In other words, we are invited to see ourselves functioning within the framework of this triad:

- The spiritual life energy, which is eternal and limitless
- The mind, which is creative as it operates in all its capacities, including logic, intuition, imagination, and creativity
- The will, which gives us independent identity and freedom of choice

By designating the will as one of these three attributes, Cayce challenges a philosophical and theological trend that is centuries old. Most great thinkers who have recognized the importance of the will have nevertheless described it as either (1) a special type of energy or (2) a particular quality of the mind. That is to say, by putting the will on an equal footing with mind and energy, Cayce asks us to reconsider and appreciate just how important it really is.

If such an analysis sounds a bit too abstract and theoretical, think about this analogy instead. In working with colors, you quickly discover that there are three primary pigments: red, blue, and yellow. You can create any other color by properly mixing two or three of the basic building blocks (for example, orange is a combination of red and yellow; brown is a mixture of all three primaries)—but blue cannot be created by combining any other colors; nor can red and yellow. Thus, these three are fundamental elements, basic ingredients.

In the same way, spiritual energy, mind, and will are the building blocks of the soul, according to Cayce. Will is not a state of mind or a type of energy. The quality it brings to human experience is fundamental. But exactly what is that quality?

Italian psychiatrist Roberto Assagioli has been one of the few modern psychotherapists who have addressed the value of the will. Assagioli founded an elaborate system of spiritual psychology called psychosynthesis, which places the will at the center of human individuality. In his book *The Act of Will*, Assagioli describes seven features that help us get a handle on how the will operates in our lives. Each feature represents a way of knowing ourselves or relating to the world around us, experiences that are missing when the will is unhealthy or inactive. These features are

- Vitality and access to dynamic energy
- Discipline and control
- Courageous initiative
- Patient persistence
- Focus and concentration
- Synthesis and harmony
- Decision making and free choice

The final item in the list is the most familiar, and, unfortunately, many theories on the will focus primarily on this one aspect alone. But Cayce—like Assagioli—attempts to expand our understanding of this faculty.

Aspects of the Will

Many qualities, not just freedom of choice, are brought into our lives by the will. These five from the Cayce readings supplement decision making—without them we would still have freedom of choice but would not be sufficiently enlightened to make wise decisions:

1. *Will gives us individuality*. This feature allows us to stand aside and observe ourselves, to be objective and self-reflective. Such self-awareness is necessary for spiritual development.
2. *Will is the opposer of habits*. We all have strong habit patterns of thinking, feeling, and acting. These ingrained

routines would control our lives if we let them. Yet, by an act of will, we can resist the momentum and steer a new course.

3. *Will is the developer of the soul*. If spiritual evolution is our goal, then right use of will is indispensable. If fact, the Cayce readings go so far as to suggest that the "whole ball game" of soul growth boils down to how we use the will.

4. *Will is the guider of the mind*. If "mind is the builder," as Cayce often stated, we're still left to wonder what directs that building process. The will provides this essential factor. By supplying an orientation, it assists the mind and ensures that the results of our creativity will be useful.

5. *Will is the agent of obedience*. In an age that teaches "Do your own thing," the notion of obedience doesn't sit well. We resist any influence that threatens our freedom. But obedience to God's will is also a factor in spiritual growth. To surrender one's own power and follow a higher purpose is an act of enlightened will.

Individual Will and Divine Will

Introducing the idea of a divine will might appear to contradict all previous points about human independence. Why should we concern ourselves with freedom and personal responsibility if ultimately there is a right way to which we must conform? Cayce's response was that we must try to live with that paradox. There are two sides of the will: one that is personally empowering and another that comes from beyond ourselves.

But the will of God is not merely a set of required choices, a mandatory road map that forbids detours. This traditional view is too limiting. No wonder that so many sincere seekers have rejected the familiar images offered for generations by traditional religions. A new view of higher will suggests that God wants us to learn how to use our freedom and exercise our independent nature, but in a way that benefits ourselves *and others*.

This point is illustrated in the story of a woman who faced painful choices in dealing with one of her children. The youngster was having problems in many areas, and any approach that seemed to offer possibilities for improvement also carried an equal threat that things could become worse for the child.

For many weeks the mother had confided in several friends and shared her confusion over the dilemma. She had prayed daily for guidance, hoping to get clear direction on what course to follow with her daughter. Yet God seemed to be silent on this issue. One day at a gathering with some of her friends who knew about the problem, she declared, "I know the will of God in this situation!" That pronouncement quickly got everyone's attention, and all were eager to hear the divine revelation. The mother's next words were a surprise to them but demonstrated profound wisdom about how God often works in our lives: "The will of God is—" She paused. "—that *I* decide."

"That *I* decide." This simple affirmation is often the key to God's will. The Creator wants us to learn how to make choices—decisions that are based on love and wisdom. Until we learn to exercise freedom of choice, we can never develop into the conscious, cocreative companions God desires.

Certainly we'll make mistakes along the way. We'll think that some of our decisions are motivated through love and insight, only to find out by the results of those choices that subtle, even unconscious forces clouded our vision. But we can learn from those errors. In fact, *how else* can we grow? We observe the same process as a child matures through adolescence and emerges as an independent, responsible adult. Without the freedom to make decisions (and, sometimes, mistakes) there is little hope for healthy development. The loving parent not only *allows* freedom of choice but *encourages* and sometimes *requires* it.

Awakening the Will

There is a second reason God wants us to learn to make decisions, related to the familiar state in which we find the human will. Symbolically speaking, our wills are usually "asleep"; most of the time they slumber, and we allow habit patterns and forces in the outside world to control us. By learning to make decisions for ourselves, we awaken the will from its sleep.

Cayce often emphasized the significance of independent decision making when he clairvoyantly counseled people about their predicaments. One young man was perplexed about how to get ahead in his career. He had recently visited a psychic medium and received the prophecy that someday a great benefactor would come into his life and financially pave the way for his success. Perhaps the news sounded too good to be true. So in his reading he asked Cayce for confirmation of this future event.

The answer might have dismayed him. He was told that the future is not predetermined. There may be probabilities and likelihoods, but everything depends on how each individual uses his or her free will. If the young man made proper decisions along the way, then such a benefactor might someday come into his life. But there were no guarantees. Destiny is a matter of what one does with the opportunities at hand.

This point of view resembles closely the one offered by Rudolf Steiner regarding human relationships. Steiner indicated that we may be destined to meet certain key individuals at particular points in our lives—meetings that are really the result of decisions made as souls even before our physical births. However, once such a meeting takes place, destiny is at an end: what remains is what we make of the opportunity with our free will.

Think about how this principle might apply to your own life. Perhaps you were destined to meet your spouse, your boss, and other significant people. But what is the quality of those relationships *now*? It's a matter not of destiny but of how you have chosen to think, feel, and act toward those individuals.

It may not please you to hear the notion that your will is usually asleep. No one likes to think he or she is "out to lunch," out of touch with what's going on in life. But even though this idea may make you uncomfortable, a little bit of careful self-observation will probably prove the point. Very rarely in the course of a day are you likely to pause and use your will. You may seem to make choices, but more often than not those "decisions" are automatic reactions, unconscious compulsions to follow old habit patterns. Circumstances probably dictate most of the direction to your typical day.

Here is a good way to test this premise. First thing in the morning, pick three goals you want to accomplish. Each one should require some initiative on your part, activities that aren't going to be completed if you merely go with the flow of the day. Then, as the day progresses, watch how easily you can get sidetracked from your intentions. For example, your mood may change. The enthusiasm and determination you felt in the morning fade as you get hungry or tired. People in your life expect you to do other things that day. Unexpected circumstances arise. You may find that the will to accomplish your three goals falls asleep and that you end up letting life around you determine how you'll use your time and energy.

Of course, sometimes you'll be successful with this experiment. You may find a careful balance between (1) commitments you've made to your goals and (2) the unanticipated needs of others. Absolute dedication to either course is an unhealthy exercise of will: On the one hand, you can become too rigid and stubborn in your insistence on fulfilling your own agenda; on the other hand, you can become so compliant to the demands of life around you that your personal will falls asleep once again. As is often the case on the spiritual path, the best way is a middle ground between two extremes.

Where does the will of God fit into all this? The divine intention is that we learn to make loving and wise choices. In so doing we develop our individualities and awaken from a symbolic sleep. However, it is just as essential to learn how to surrender to something bigger than ourselves. This is the paradox of spiritual power: we must exercise our freedom of choice and in so doing grow in personal strength, *but* we must also be able to give it all up and surrender to a higher power.

How can we learn to surrender? How can we give ourselves *over* to God without feeling that we are giving *up* or giving *in?* The very idea of surrender connotes capitulation and submission. Who wants to be a weakling or a wimp?

Cayce suggested that we learn a higher form of surrender through *fasting*. But what does a starvation diet have to do with spirituality? True fasting is more than just a limited food intake, it means letting go of your willfulness about something. It *might* be the amount of food you desire, but it could just as easily be *any desire pattern:* the amount of television you watch, the frequency of your critical comments, how often you insist on winning arguments. By practicing this sort of fasting, we can learn to turn willfulness into willingness. That's the quality God needs from us in order to work creatively in our lives.

Working with Your Will

Once we have a deeper understanding of the dual nature of the will and its importance to spiritual growth, we can focus on making day-to-day choices. Even though the topic of will encompasses much more than decision making, that's generally where we face the issue most often and most directly.

The making of a decision is a three-step process that is influenced by the timing of the sequence and the intensity we feel at various stages of the progression.

1. *Confusion.* In moments when we initially face a choice, there is usually a feeling of confusion or ambiguity (otherwise we really wouldn't face a decision). Without some degree of disorientation, the situation would simply be an imperative awaiting implementation.

   The confusion we encounter in the face of a real decision is produced by the competing voices of the alternatives. One voice promises a certain outcome; another warns against the first and offers its own picture of the best course. It might be easier to reach a decision if only two voices competed, but often there are several.

   Just remember that it's okay to be confused; it's natural and even healthy. People who never get bewildered probably aren't growing very much. The confusion can indicate that former ways of seeing life are giving way to new understandings. From among all the possibilities, you'll have a chance to create your future with your decision.

2. *Identification of options.* Not every voice that speaks during the first step will propose a viable course of action. A preliminary level of decision making must take place at this second step, one that narrows the field to a few serious candidates. Sometimes the will can be used skillfully at this stage to combine two or more similar alternatives and thereby create a new option.

3. *A decision in favor of one option.* This is the stage at which the choice is made. Even though more than one alternative

may be appealing, your will makes it possible to focus on only one and commit your energies to it. That decision doesn't have to be forever, but for the time being it must exclude any competing options. Your decision should be one of commitment to action. By your choice you say to yourself (and often to the outside world as well), "Here's what I think is best. I'm going to act on my choice and walk some steps down that path. I'll be watching for results and may need to alter my course later. But for now, this is my intention."

As simple as this three-step process may sound, there are still some pitfalls. One is to rush the sequence. (This is especially a problem if we believe that it's wrong or unspiritual to be confused.) In our haste to reach a decision, we may not give ourselves a chance to find the best alternative and thus end up re-creating the themes and patterns of our past.

Another pitfall is to get stuck at the first or second stage. We may get mired in the confusion, never emerging from what started out as a healthy examination of alternatives. Or we may get so caught up in the identification of all those choices that we never get around to deciding on just one.

A third pitfall is trying to skip a step, especially the second one. Confusion and disorientation can be painful, and in our discomfort we may be tempted to seize the first option that comes along. It takes courage to withstand the tension and uncertainty and allow sufficient time to arrive at several alternatives.

However, with patience and understanding, we can carefully and consciously move through this three-part progression with any decision we face. The amount of time necessary will vary depending on the situation. A medical emergency will probably create a moment of panic and confusion; however, one must recognize the alternative courses of action and choose one fairly quickly. The sequence may be completed in a matter of seconds.

By contrast, a person who is going through a divorce will probably be confused for weeks or months, maybe longer. The bewilderment is natural and should be seen as healthy, indicating that many inner changes are taking place. Then comes a period of identifying alternative life-styles—remaining single, perhaps, or looking for opportunities to form a new romantic relationship. It may be tempting to grab the first alternative that comes along, but with courage one can allow the time necessary for several options to present themselves more clearly. When one finally arrives at a choice, the decision may have been months or even years in the making.

No matter how short or long the time required, decisions are undoubtedly exciting. The freedom to choose allows us to feel alive. What a privilege! In fact, Cayce indicated that many other dimensions of consciousness don't allow as much liberty as we experience in the physical world. In many of the realms to which we may pass after bodily death, we live out the consequences of decisions we made during our earthly lives, but without as much direct access to free will. Souls often reincarnate into the physical world to reconnect with their wills and make needed changes.

Take the time to appreciate this extraordinary spiritual gift. Your will is the key to your future. God wants you to use it to make wise and loving decisions. Today you'll have many chances to do just that.

EXERCISE

There are big and there are little decisions that you make every day. Consciously go through the three steps of decision making with one issue today. Pick a situation for which the following sequence can be completed in a single day without having to hurry or skip any of the three steps. Move through these stages:

1. *Confusion*—the chaos or disorganization that creates the need for a solution to be decided on
2. *Alternatives*—the various possibilities and alternative solutions one discovers
3. *Choice*—the act of will that selects one of the alternatives and makes a commitment to act

Observe any tendency to fall "asleep" during the process, to let habits from the past or the will of someone else decide for you. Then make your choice, commit yourself to acting on it, and watch for results as you apply your decision.

PRINCIPLE #15

In Every Moment We Are Either Helping or Hurting

A wealthy English nobleman and his daughter were walking one day down the sordid streets of Calcutta. All around them were filth and unspeakable poverty. The young girl was unable to take her eyes off the panorama of suffering. Her father, however, focused straight ahead as if oblivious to his surroundings. At last the daughter tugged at her father's sleeve and pleaded, "Daddy, do something for these people. They're so poor!" Without hesitation the nobleman snapped at his child, "There's nothing I can do. Besides, I didn't make them poor."

Upon hearing such a story, we may feel indignant toward the insensitive nobleman. Or we may empathize with his sense of helplessness at facing such an awesome problem. We may even want to join him in his denial of responsibility, to say with him, "I didn't make them poor."

Every day we are exposed to an array of human suffering that can bewilder and dismay us. What's a body to do? How can one person make a difference? Faced with this dilemma, we seem to have only a few choices. We can allow ourselves to become overwhelmed with guilt and despair, or we can declare our noninvolvement, saying in effect, "It's not my responsibility."

Yet the Cayce readings indicate that there is another option, one that calls us to action and involvement as it delivers us from a sense of powerlessness to act against overwhelming odds. This option invites us to do what we can to fulfill a need and then leave the results to the Creator. Even when our best attempt seems ineffective, we can trust that our effort makes a difference—that it counts in ways we may not see.

Our Temptation toward Neutrality

What is our first thought when we hear that two of our friends are having a quarrel? Do we immediately look for a way to avoid getting involved? What do we think when we see a news story about a major natural disaster? It's normal to feel relieved that we don't live there. When we learn about a crime victim, do we wonder, How can I protect myself from such a fate? These reactions are typical; they express the fundamental desire for self-preservation. Yet from a spiritual perspective they suggest that we're running away from our special opportunities.

Life engages us every day with opportunities to express the love of the Creator. Most situations involve other people. As the Cayce readings often commented, we neither live nor die unto ourselves. Rather, we live in constant association with the rest of life. Our actions and even our thoughts have a constant impact on all of creation.

In every situation we encounter, we have a choice of options. We can try to make things better, or we can let things slide. But each choice makes an impact on the course of human events. As one popular aphorism states: "If you're not part of the solution, you're part of the problem." In other words, there's no such thing as neutral ground.

We Are Responsible to One Another

When problems challenge us to take a stand, why isn't it possible to find a truly neutral position? No story underscores this predicament more dramatically than that of the life of Albert Speer, a brilliant young German architect beginning his career in the chaotic decade after World War I. Through a series of seemingly random encounters, he found himself employed as Adolf Hitler's master builder. In his autobiography, *Inside the Third Reich*, Speer comments on Hitler's almost hypnotic power over the members of his inner circle, Speer included. Eventually, during the war, Speer was promoted to armaments minister. In that post he was single-handedly responsible for the continued industrial output of Germany's war machine. This job carried with it an immeasurable amount of pressure that soon absorbed all of Speer's mental and physical energy.

One day late in the war Speer's friend Karl Hanke paid him a visit. Speer had known Hanke for several years and considered him an individual of integrity and compassion. The visitor was tremendously upset and squirmed uneasily on his chair. Finally he muttered to Speer, "If you ever get an invitation to inspect a concentration camp in Upper Silesia, don't do it." He said he'd seen things there that he was not permitted to describe and, in fact, *could* not describe.

In his book, Speer admits that in that moment he became *personally* responsible for the horrors of Auschwitz, for he had been presented with a choice, and he chose to turn a deaf ear. He had work to do, and he *didn't want to know* what was going on. Says Speer, "From that moment on, I was inescapably contaminated morally; from fear of discovering something which might have made me turn from my course, I had closed my eyes. . . . Because I failed at that time, I still feel, to this day, responsible for Auschwitz in a wholly personal sense."

However, when most of Hitler's entourage continued later to blindly follow his ravings, even to the point of practically destroying all of Germany to slow the Allied advance, Speer awakened to his responsibilities. He began to defy the Führer openly and even conceived an assassination plot. Commenting on his plan to kill his friend and leader, Speer observed that he'd spent years in the company of murderers and yet didn't realize how their influence had affected him until he himself began to contemplate murder.

Clearly this story shows that no one can stand passively on the sidelines. Each of us is responsible at every moment for making a difference one way or another. Our choices may not seem to address issues of life and death, as did those of Speer, but the spiritual law is the same no matter what the scale. We are either helping or hurting at every moment.

As Cayce told a young woman in 1932, our every act and thought either adds to the bringing about of God's kingdom or prevents it from being manifested in the material plane, for all of us are God's agents as we travel through life.

Yes, But Do My Little Efforts Really Count?

You may have heard of or sung the hymn about everyone lighting just one little candle to make a brighter world. But what if no one else lights a candle? Would the fact that you lit yours still make a difference?

Speer definitely made a difference when he labored frantically to prevent the wholesale destruction of Germany's countryside, as ordered by Hitler. Yet it's naive to assume that even in his powerful position as armaments minister he could have done anything to lessen appreciably the horror of the Holocaust. So why did he feel responsible? Should he have? The answer is yes. From the spiritual perspective, attitudes and actions can have a tremendous influence, even when they're considered insignificant from a material angle.

In 1925 Edgar Cayce volunteered a short addition to a dream interpretation reading. There had been a major disaster in China that had killed a great number of people, he explained, and he went on to say that many of those recently departed souls had taken up a position in the spiritual realm that would radically influence the development of that nation in the coming years. In other words, the attitudes and desires of those souls were continuing to have an impact on human affairs, possibly a *greater* impact because of their position in the spiritual plane.

This is a novel idea, implying as it does that we each wield a greater power at the mental and spiritual levels than we realize. But we don't have to wait until we leave the physical body at death to claim that power! Our actions count, as do our attitudes and thoughts. Once we recognize this, we can no longer say, "There's nothing I can do; it's not my responsibility." Everything that life brings to us is our responsibility. There's always something we can do, even if it's just to care. Remember that there's a difference between being responsible *for* and being responsible *to*. Even when we aren't to blame personally for a problem or crisis, we are still capable of constructive response.

Small Can Be Powerful

A popular aphorism reminds us, "It's impossible to know the power of just one kind word." In the same spirit, philosopher E. F. Schumacher coined the phrase "Small is beautiful," and the renowned Russian acting teacher Konstantin Stanislavski was fond of saying, "There are no small parts, only small actors."

How can we understand this principle, that small is important? For centuries most of the evidence seemed to support the opposite contention—that larger is always better, whether the subject is hammers, individuals, or nations. In fact, that's not always the case. In modern times, more and more people appreciate the value of smallness, a shift in attitude that has come about largely because of science. For example, the microchip has changed countless aspects of our life-style. Using minuscule amounts of electricity to store and process information, this tiny invention has revolutionized virtually every aspect of modern life. The miniaturization of technology is a major cultural force in our times.

As may often be the case, natural science discovers and validates phenomena in the outer world that are equally valid in the inner world of mind and spirit. As surely as the tiniest microelectronic equipment is often the most valuable, so may a single action or word influence an individual's entire development.

We've all had experiences with just how potent a small deed or a few simple words can be. A twelve-year-old boy growing up in a small southern town developed a passing fascination with Oriental martial arts. One night he was in his bedroom, practicing kicks against the door. Eventually, satisfied that he was ready for greater challenges, he decided to try his kicks against the wall. He learned something about house construction when his foot went through the plasterboard that separated his bedroom from his closet.

The boy was petrified with fear. He couldn't even imagine the wrath that he would earn by destroying the very walls of his house. His face blanched and solemn, he went to his father and said, "Dad, I have to tell you something that I've done." Perplexed and slightly concerned, the father inquired further.

The boy stoically led his dad back to the scene of the "crime" and stood beside the evidence. Bracing for the worst, the boy was surprised to hear his father laugh and say, "I can fix that."

To the father this was just another little incident in the daily parade that comprised the trials and joys of being a parent. But to the boy, who had trembled with guilt and fear, his response was nothing less than a firsthand experience of deliverance and divine mercy. And although the father forgot the event within days, it continued to live in the boy's memory, contributing to the development of his character even as an adult.

We never know how much impact we have on others. Even our casual remarks may have a resounding influence on someone. An exchange, though brief and seemingly insignificant, may profoundly affect a person's future. Edgar Cayce's life was thus affected by his brief encounter with Arthur Lammers. In 1923 Cayce was a professional photographer who served occasionally as a "psychic diagnostician." In other words, he was applying his psychic gift part-time and only for medical information.

One day Arthur Lammers showed up on his doorstep and asked Cayce for a psychic reading on his horoscope. This sounded odd to Cayce, but he agreed to let Lammers ask the questions once he was in a trance. The information that followed contained the first reference in a Cayce reading to the concept of reincarnation. From that small event, Cayce's life and work took on dramatic new directions. The entire legacy of his spiritual information can be traced back to that insignificant request made by a single passing character.

The Law of Resonance

Another way to understand your effect on others is through the law of resonance. To illustrate, imagine that you have in each hand a tuning fork of the same pitch. Rap one tuning fork against a hard surface to make it ring; then, as it vibrates, bring it close to the similar fork in your other hand. As you do this, you will discover that the second tuning fork begins to ring as well, even without being struck directly. The vibrations of the one fork *stimulate* the vibrations of the other. This is known as resonance.

The law of resonance works with people, too. Your thoughts and attitudes at every moment radiate outward, influencing the thoughts of others. Of course, the process operates the opposite way, too. Although you may not be conscious of how it works, your own feelings, moods, and thoughts are influenced by others. The key word is *influenced,* which is considerably different from *controlled.* Each of us has free will to choose our mental states, but the influence that comes from other people—even through an invisible process of resonance—makes it *easier and more likely* to choose certain emotions and attitudes over others.

Are you responsible for the thoughts and actions of others? No. Each individual has the power to think and act according to his or her own decisions. However, you *are* responsible for your *own* thoughts and actions, which have an impact on everyone in the world. And you are responsible *to* other people to help them through your positive, constructive state of mind.

When asked how to have an impact on world conditions, Cayce responded that small groups can have far more influence than might be expected. The prayers *and* right actions of a few dedicated individuals can change the course of events in the world. Once Cayce even suggested that a single person can alter what is happening in a city.

What mysterious process could validate Cayce's promise? Was he referring to mind control, a dedicated prayer group overpowering the anger and aggression of soldiers or crazed leaders? Surely not. Psychic manipulation would have violated the law of free will for each soul.

Perhaps "resonance" is a better answer. People who are praying *and* living with a positive spirit are capable of producing a vibratory pattern just as real as the one from a tuning fork that has just been struck. For example, anyone in the world who is caught up in a war but has a desire for peace and understanding will be like a second tuning fork: that person will find it easier to choose peace and understanding even in the midst of tense, hostile circumstances. The small, seemingly insignificant efforts of even a few dozen people may be influential enough to affect millions of others.

But What Should I Do?

Cayce's suggestion to "live as you pray" is good advice, but translating that into something more specific is a very personal matter that must be determined by each individual. Many needs and admirable causes beckon for our attention, and each of us has to decide where and how to take action.

For example, suppose you have a concern about the environment. You may have heard that rain forests are being indiscriminately cut down to grow crops that in turn feed cattle to provide cheap beef for our fast-food restaurants. Or perhaps you're disturbed by the fact that gasoline and other fossil fuels are polluting the air. And you may have read reports that chlorofluorocarbons (released into the atmosphere by the use of air conditioners and in the manufacture of Styrofoam) are eroding the ozone layer. Suppose you care about all these issues. Where do you begin? Do you stop eating hamburgers? Do you quit driving cars? Do you boycott all Styrofoam products or disconnect your air conditioner?

If you try to take every possible action, you will probably begin to *resent* the restrictions you've placed on yourself. Furthermore, it's virtually impossible to live in this technological world without contributing in *some measure* to its damaging influence on the environment. So should you just give up in despair? No. It's important to remember that with whatever positive efforts you can make, you *can* make a difference.

Consider the operation of a car's steering wheel. There is a range in which the wheel effectively steers the car. Even a slight rotation of just a few degrees will eventually shift the car into a new lane that may be more suitable for travel. But if the wheel is turned too sharply while the car is moving, it can cause the car to flip over and crash.

With that in mind, get involved in the issues that most concern you. Select actions that would be akin to turning the steering wheel gently, effectively. What's right for one person won't necessarily be right for someone else. One person concerned about the rain forests may choose to boycott all fast-food restaurants; another may simply choose not to eat hamburgers; and yet another may just want to *cut down* on the number of hamburgers eaten. These actions all address the problem within the range of what individuals can do without throwing their lives seriously out of whack. What you do and how much you do about your concerns are determined by your own conscience. Allow yourself to be stretched and even inconvenienced, but if guilt or resentment follows, you've probably gone beyond what's best for you right now.

What Would God Have Me Do?

You are either helping or hurting at every moment. No sitting on the fence, no neutral ground. Something in your soul probably responds, "Then I want to help; I want to be supportive on the side of healing and creativity."

Admittedly, you know that you won't be able to maintain that orientation every moment of every day. However, as often as possible, you want your efforts—big and small—to make a positive contribution. Exactly *how* can you do it? How can you meet situations in your daily life as a wise, effective helper? Sometimes it isn't easy to see what to do when the dilemmas of daily living arise.

The Cayce readings offer a strategy for anyone who really wants to help in the world. First you must make the unavoidable choice we face many times in a single day: whether to care. You start to become an active force for good simply by taking the time and making the decision to care.

The second choice is a matter of deciding how you can make a difference. This is far more complicated, but if you're sincere in your desire to help, the "how" will be shown to you.

Cayce often advised individuals to ask sincerely, What would God have me do? Ask this question silently two or three times and then remain quiet and listen. You needn't expect to hear an audible voice. Rather, if you genuinely and consistently seek this guidance, it will eventually become clear. Then, as you *apply* what you are led and inspired to do, you become a helper whose impact travels in both visible and invisible ways.

EXERCISE

This exercise will focus your awareness on the subtle ways in which your input to the world around you isn't neutral. Either it's constructive and life-affirming *or* it's destructive and life-denying. The choice is yours, many times daily.

Spend one day keeping in the mind the premise that you *can* make a difference. Pay attention to the *little things* in life and how you can have an impact on the world around you. Take time to care about people and about the quality of how you respond to situations. Try to build hope, self-esteem, and understanding by your thoughts, words, and deeds.

PRINCIPLE #16

Love Means Honoring the Other Person's Free Will

A contemporary proverb says, "If you love something, set it free. If it doesn't come back, it was never yours to begin with." However, a recent bumper sticker put an interesting twist on this slogan by changing the ending to "If it doesn't come back, hunt it down and kill it." To some people such a parody may be amusing; to others it may be offensive. However this satire may strike you, it is an unfortunate truth that many human beings confuse love with domination and control. In the name of love parents have smothered their children, lovers have tethered their partners, and entire cultures have been reduced to slavery. All this under the battle cry "I only want what's best for you." Why is this? What is it about the human heart that can so distort the impulse of love as to turn it into bondage? To answer this important question, we must look carefully at three factors: power, control, and free will.

Power and control are unambiguous. Power is the energy and influence to get things done, whether we're talking about horsepower, atomic power, or political power. Control is the exertion of power over something or someone. We've probably all had the experience of controlling and being controlled.

But what is free will, and who has it? Throughout the centuries these questions have been hotly debated—and not just by scholars but also by ordinary people who stop and observe life. A Sunday school teacher once asked her high school class, "Do animals have free will?" All of them said yes. One student explained, "When a cat's hungry, it eats; if it's not, it won't. The cat exercises its freedom of choice."

This was a fairly good answer, but it missed the point. The cat is only obeying the physical laws of hunger. Will the cat, when hungry, offer its food out of compassion to another cat that is hungrier still? There is no evidence to validate this, except perhaps in the case of a mother cat with her kittens, and that is just another example of natural instinct. In short, a cat does just what nature directs it to do: It follows its instincts, which are born of the two laws of nature—protection of self and protection of the species. In the kingdom of nature there is no question of free will. All creatures march to the laws of creation.

Human beings are different. We are more than mere creatures of the earth. It's true, of course, that as physical beings we share the primal instincts. But that's only our surface identity. At a deeper level we are spiritual beings—souls who are *children of God*—each with an inner source of the Creative Spirit. Unfortunately, our two natures—spiritual and physical—do not always cooperate. To make matters worse, we can easily use our spiritual power to create monstrous exaggerations of our physical desires. As the Cayce readings often warn us, we have the power to create either crimes or miracles. What determines which we create?

Power and Responsibility

We all have plenty of opportunities in life to feel powerless. You may start out the door one morning and discover that your brand-new car won't start. Unless you're a skilled auto mechanic, you'll probably feel helpless. Or you may get laid off suddenly from your job and painfully experience how powerless you are in your work life. Getting sick is another way to encounter directly the feeling of powerlessness. There's nothing like a good case of the flu to make one feel totally vulnerable.

In spite of these examples, the fact is that we always have power, much more than most of us realize. Scientific research indicates that the typical human being uses only a tiny fraction of the potential power of the brain. What would it be like to have at your command the *full* power of your brain? The following story may provide a clue.

During the few years in the late 1920s and early 1930s when

the Cayce Hospital was operating successfully, its staff and friends would gather on Sunday and listen to lectures on the various topics addressed in Cayce's psychic readings. On February 15, 1931, Cayce himself gave a short talk on mental telepathy. In that presentation he shared an experience or, more accurately, an experiment he'd conducted years earlier as a young man. He had been giving readings for several years and had been puzzling over the extraordinary power that evidently resided in the subconscious mind. In a moment of hubris Cayce boasted to a friend, "I can force an individual to come to me." She said, "That's impossible," to which he replied, "I'll prove it to you. Before tomorrow at twelve o'clock, your brother will not only come up here, but he will ask me to do something for him." This was an ambitious boast, because the woman's brother did not like Cayce and had no sympathy for his psychic work.

The next morning at ten o'clock Cayce sat quietly in his office chair, focusing his mind on the girl's brother. After about half an hour of concentrated thought Cayce saw him pass by on the street below, then turn and come up onto the steps of his studio. The man stood there a few minutes, looked up the steps, then walked back out. In a few minutes he turned in again, and this time he came up the steps to the second floor.

His sister was amazed to see him. "What are you doing here?" she asked. He sat on the edge of the table, turning his hat in his hands, and finally answered, "Well, I hardly know, but I had some trouble last night at the shop, and, well, you've been telling me so much about Mr. Cayce, I just wondered if he couldn't help me out."

According to Cayce, the sister almost fainted when she heard those words. Then, for good measure, he demonstrated the same power on another acquaintance the following day. Yet after those experiences he decided never to do such a thing again. Why? Because he realized it involved using his sacred gift to impose his will on another. In his 1931 lecture Cayce insisted that to control another person mentally is related to the "black arts." He continued, "For, as our information says, anyone who would force another to submit to his will is a tyrant!"

Correction without Coercion

Questions of love, control, and freedom are probably nowhere as pronounced as in families, especially in relations between parents and children. Many people came to Cayce asking for advice on how to rear their offspring. One of their primary concerns was discipline—how much and in what form? Although the readings certainly recognized the need to guide and direct children, they consistently discouraged the types of discipline that would break a child's will.

One couple dealing with their child's "stubborn, fresh, and disobedient attitude" asked in a reading, "Would you advise scolding or hitting him when he is so uncontrollable? Or what method would you advise?" Cayce's answer was typical: Patience, kindness, and gentleness should always be the method used, not scolding or tormenting the child.

Decades later a businessman acquainted with Cayce's philosophy of child rearing observed an all-too-familiar example of its opposite. Traveling in an airplane, he found himself sitting in front of a family of five—two parents and three children. During the long flight the children were completely wild. They cried, fussed, screamed, and ran down the aisle. The father added to this chaos by constantly scolding them. "No!! I'll smack you! I'll tan your bottom! Be quiet, I mean it!" All his threats did nothing but contribute to the disruption.

Certainly most of us can remember a teacher from our school days who commanded our respect without ever raising his or her voice. What creates the difference? How can one person have such quiet yet unmistakable authority while another fails to command respect despite a domineering personality?

Of course, children themselves differ, but the greatest factor in maintaining discipline seems to relate to the inner life of the parent or instructor. In 1932 a couple came to Cayce for advice concerning their adolescent children, who had a negative attitude toward school, preferring to play or even get a job rather than continue their education. The parents wondered if they should force their children to continue their formal education. The reading refrained from giving a simple yes or no. Instead, it encouraged the parents to look more closely at their *own* attitudes toward education and determine whether their children were simply following the parents' lead. Perhaps the parents had built into the attitudes of the children a dislike for formal education by what they'd said before the children ever began attending school.

The most effective way to lead or direct *anyone* is to accept the guidance and discipline of your own spiritual ideal. For example, a forty-three-year-old woman was suffering through a painful relationship with her mother. She sought help from Cayce and in her reading asked several questions about how to improve that relationship. She wondered how to create more harmony between them. Cayce's answer was for her to create a harmonious condition within herself. However, the woman persisted with questions about her mother, and Cayce continued gently to bring her back to the true focus, which was to live and be the ideal of harmony within the self. This was the best help she could give her mother. For no one can live another's life, Cayce said, or think for another.

Even in the area of healing prayer, the readings cautioned against imposing one's will upon others. Suppose someone you love is suffering from an addiction such as alcoholism. You want to help, but how? Prayer is certainly one action you can take. But if this loved one is not yet interested in changing, what form of prayer is best? Cayce described two kinds: direct and protective. In *direct* prayer you ask for a *specific* healing to take place. Such a prayer is appropriate only if the target of your prayer has asked for such efforts. In that case you are adding energy to a process of change that he or she has already willed. If the person for whom you're praying is not in sympathy with your efforts, direct prayer may in fact aggravate the problem. In such a case *protective* prayer is best. With this type of prayer, ask that the person be surrounded and protected by the forces of love and healing while at the same time allowing that individual his or her own free will in choosing whether to change.

Is It Ever Appropriate to Take a Stand?

One concern should be addressed in this area of free will. What are the boundaries? Should we let one person persecute another in the name of free will, for example, allow a man to beat his wife or a sovereign nation to enslave its people? Of course not. The divine gift of free will does not entitle an individual to impose that will on another. Moral civilizations are built on mutually accepted laws designed to prevent such abuses of power.

There are times when we must take a stand against someone's willfulness, even when we love that individual. In 1934 a forty-eight-year-old mother had a series of readings from Cayce. She was seeking advice on a complicated and difficult problem: Her grown daughter had left an unhappy marriage and returned home with her young son. The woman had many questions about how to bring about a resolution to this troubled situation. The reading generally encouraged her to release her anxieties, since she had done all she could for the moment. The parties involved needed to work out the problem for themselves. Yet one question the woman asked was whether the husband should be brought to court and forced to pay child support. The reading advised that mother and daughter appeal first to the husband's sense of duty *and privilege* in caring for the boy. Out of care and respect for the father, they were to give him another chance to freely choose to fulfill of his duties. However, if he continued to refuse, the reading counseled taking him to court.

Power and Restraint

One way to evaluate the maturity of a culture is to observe how its leaders wield power. How are those who are already strong kept in check, and how are the weaker ones protected? The laws and practices that address these issues reflect the fair-mindedness of the people. For example, at a brute physical level, men are generally stronger than women. Because of this physiological fact, some cultures have reduced women to mere possessions. Early stages of Western civilization leaned in this direction, creating an orientation that is slow to change even now.

However, in the twelveth century a new consciousness began to dawn, reflected in the love poetry of the troubadours. Suddenly women gained new status and were entitled to protection under the new code of chivalry. It became the duty and privilege of every good knight to honor, serve, and protect the fairer, though more delicate, sex.

In addition to battling evil and protecting the weak, the code of chivalry defined the appropriate responses in a love relationship. Suddenly women had as much say in affairs as men, with equal rights to exercise their free will. This new awareness emerges in the legends of King Arthur and his knights of the Round Table. The story "Sir Gawain's Marriage," as recounted in *Bulfinch's Mythology*, is an excellent illustration.

The tale begins with King Arthur battling a villain in defense of a damsel in distress. However, this particularly evil knight fought unfairly by enchanting the battleground so that is sapped Arthur's strength. After defeating Arthur, the knight offered him a choice: He could either die on the spot or be given a riddle that he'd have a year to solve. If by that time he failed to answer the riddle correctly, he would forfeit all his lands and possessions to the knight. Arthur chose the latter route and heard the riddle: What is it that women most desire?

In the months that followed Arthur sought far and wide for the answer. He discovered many possible solutions: precious jewels, rich lands, a handsome knight in marriage. He wondered, however, if any of those answers were correct. Finally, the year was over and Arthur was duty-bound to return to the wicked knight and do his best to answer the riddle. Moping along through a forest on his way to the test site, he spied the ugliest hag he had ever seen. Descriptions would fail to convey her monstrosity. To avoid any contact with her, Arthur moved to the opposite side of the road and pretended not to notice her. However, as he passed, the woman called out to him by name and said, "I see that you consider me too ugly to greet, but I may possess something that you most desire!"

Her words aroused Arthur's interest, and he inquired further. She said, "I know the answer to the riddle you have been given, and I will tell it to you on one condition. If it proves correct, you will marry me to a knight of your court."

Arthur was uncomfortable about making such a promise, but he agreed to the condition. The hag thereupon declared that women most desire *their own will*.

This answer proved correct and rescued Arthur from his dilemma. He returned to Camelot amid great shouts of joy, but when he told the full story, the joy turned to lamentation. Arthur sadly asked which knight would volunteer to marry the hag and fulfill his pledge. All the knights lowered their faces and averted their eyes. Finally Gawain, out of love for his king, stepped forward. The hag was ushered to court, where amid great wailing the two were married by the bishop. After a doleful wedding feast, the entire court, including the newlyweds, retired for the night.

Gawain courageously led his bride to their nuptial chamber, whereupon they prepared for bed. However, as Gawain turned from removing his armor, he was shocked to discover standing in the room the most beautiful woman he'd ever seen. After a moment of numbed silence, he stammered, "Wh-who are you?"

The woman replied, "I am your new bride! I had been under a spell, and because you married me willingly, the spell has been partially removed. I can now be my true beautiful self for exactly half of every day."

She then posed this thorny question: "Which half of the day do you wish me to be beautiful?"

After pretending to think a moment, Gawain declared that he preferred her to be beautiful at night when they shared a bed together. The woman conceded that Gawain's choice was reasonable but asked him to consider the issue from her point of view. Couldn't he see that she would rather be beautiful during the day, as she interacted socially with the rest of the court?

Reflecting on this test of his love, Gawain replied, "Woman, it shall be as you will." Whereupon the bride joyously announced that because he had given her freedom of choice, the spell had been completely broken and she could now be her beautiful self both day *and* night! This charming tale ends with the couplet, "And Gawain kissed that lady fair, lying upon the sheet; And swore as he was a true knight, the spice never was so sweet."

True love is never possessive, never controlling, never manipulative. Instead, it is honest, cooperative, and liberating. Above all, loving another means granting that person—whether child, parent, lover, or friend—the right to exercise the divine gift of free will.

EXERCISE

Take an audit of your close personal relationships. Who are the people you love most? Take a few moments and reflect on your feelings and attitudes about those individuals. Out of love and care, is there someone for whom you have particular concern because he or she may be living in what you consider a misguided way? Do you find that you often want to intervene with advice or even control? You may have the best of intentions, but try changing that reaction on your part.

For several days experiment with a different way of being with that individual. Keep as your number one priority in that relationship a respect for this individual's free will. Give the person space to make his or her own choices. Be supportive even if that person's decisions aren't what you'd want. Try expressing your love for this individual by honoring more deeply his or her independence and freedom.

PRINCIPLE #17

Compassion Is a Way of Seeing and Knowing

A Jewish folk tale—included in William R. White's *Stories for Telling*—recounts the story of a grieving widow whose only son had just died in a tragic accident. Desperate with sorrow, the woman went to a holy man, seeking to employ his magic. "Please, bring my son back to life," she pleaded. "Surely you have the power to persuade the Almighty to heal my broken heart."

The wise man sat in silence for a moment and then said gently, "Bring me a mustard seed from a home that has never known sorrow. I will use that seed to heal your grief."

Bolstered by this promise, the widow immediately set out on her quest. She went first to the wealthiest home in the village. Surely the sorrows of life have passed by this house, she thought. As a woman opened the door, the widow announced, "I am in search of a home that has never known sorrow. Have I found such a place?"

The hostess stared at her with tortured eyes and finally cried, "You have come to the wrong house!" Inviting the widow into her home, she began to describe in detail all the tragedies that had touched her family. The widow stayed with the woman several days, comforting and consoling her.

After she departed, the widow continued her quest, but wherever she went, from estate to hovel, she found lives beset with sorrow and pain. The stories and people touched her heart. Always she listened with sympathy and understanding and did what she could to ease their grief.

Eventually she forgot entirely her quest for the magic mus-

157

tard seed. Yet through her compassion, her heart had indeed been healed of its wound.

What Is Compassion?

The widow was healed of her grief through the miracle of compassion. But what is compassion? Technically, it means "to suffer with." Having compassion means sharing in the feelings of others and having a desire to help them. Poetically, it has often been described as a condition of the heart. One who is compassionate has a soft, gentle, or bleeding heart. One who is *not* compassionate has a hard heart, a heart of stone, or no heart at all!

We might go further and say that compassion is a way of perceiving, an avenue of authentic knowledge. The epistemology (theory of how knowledge is obtained) found in the Cayce readings leaves room for both head *and* heart to serve as vehicles for knowing. Appreciating this idea may require a new perspective on ourselves. We're familiar with the way in which careful, systematic *thinking* leads to discovery and insight, but feelings are usually considered subjective and personal. When it comes to understanding the world around us objectively, the modern approach ignores our feeling nature. Cayce and other sources challenge us to experience how feelings—especially compassion and love—are instruments through which can we receive reliable information about ourselves and others.

Edgar Cayce was a man of compassion. This is most evident in the portion of his legacy that has never been published: his extensive correspondence. Although overshadowed by his remarkable psychic discourses, his letters bear the imprint of a man who cared deeply about the struggles and sufferings of other people.

It would be easy to imagine Cayce solely as "the great psychic," distant and emotionally detached from those who sought his help. Such an image is particularly tempting when we recognize that he never even met the majority of people who obtained readings; the requests were more often mailed in, and the party received a transcript of the reading. But if Cayce couldn't meet all the people who asked him for help, he could write to them—and this resulted in a huge collection of Cayce's personal letters to these people. In an age when long-distance phone calls were a rarity, carefully thought-out letters were a frequent way to reach out to friends. Someday Cayce's letters may be published, as have those of Jung and other significant figures. They will provide an important balance in how the world sees and remembers Edgar Cayce, for not only was he a man of extraordinary thinking and an individual of outstanding intuitive and clairvoyant mental accomplishments, he was also—and equally important—a man of compassion and caring.

A History of Compassion

Study any culture and you will find compassion to be a prime virtue. Even in the ancient cuneiform and hieroglyphic writings of Sumer and Egypt we find the idea that good government and compassion are connected. The Sumerian king Ur-Nammu in the third millennium B.C. saw to it "that the orphan did not fall prey to the wealthy, that the widow did not fall prey to the powerful, that the man of one shekel [a monetary unit] did not fall prey to the man of sixty shekels."

The pharaohs of ancient Egypt believed that at death they faced a judgment. Their *Book of the Dead* gave instructions on how to pass over into the afterlife. In part they were to say, "I hurt no servant with his master. I cause no famine. I cause no weeping. I am not an adulterer. I am not a murderer. I give not orders for murder. I cause not suffering to men."

Of course, true compassion is more than just following rules or laws; it's a state of the heart. But the very creation of those laws shows a sensitivity to the feelings and needs of others. They are also evidence of a sincere desire to improve conditions. The laws of justice are born of compassion.

The Bible has nearly a hundred references to compassion. Some affirm God's profound care for us; others instruct us to show compassion to one another. For example, Zechariah (7:9) declares, "Thus says the Lord of hosts: Render true judgements, show kindness and mercy to one another." The New Testament book of Colossians (3:12) makes the same plea: "Clothe yourselves with compassion, kindness, humility, meekness, and patience."

Many of Eastern religions also assert the importance of compassion. Upon reaching complete enlightenment under the

Bodhi tree, the Buddha returned from his inner journey with a new vision. He recognized that all suffering is born of selfishness and that the antidote is compassion.

There are two great schools of Buddhism. The older of the two, Therevada, requires its closest adherents to follow an ascetic life. In this branch, the historical Buddha maintains a central position and the psychology of personal salvation is emphasized. Its ideal is the Arhat, or "worthy one," who has attained blissful nirvana through the eradication of karma.

In contrast, the Mahayana school permits its most devoted followers to maintain relatively normal social roles. The historic Buddha is deeply revered but is seen as one incarnation of an eternal, cosmic Buddha. The ideal of Mahayana Buddhism is the bodhisattva, one who reaches total enlightenment yet chooses to postpone for the sake of others his well-deserved transition to nirvana. Out of compassion a bodhisattva remains involved with the earth experience, continuing to work for the enlightenment of every sentient being.

Jesus expressed the same desire when he referred to his impending death: "And I, when I am lifted up from the earth, will draw all people to myself" (John 12:32). In fact, many Christian theologians see the very purpose of the crucifixion as a divine gesture of compassion that is intended to awaken the same quality in the human heart.

Cayce's philosophy and psychology seem to belong to the Mahayana school rather than the Therevada school. For example, Cayce often encouraged people to stay involved in traditional life challenges, suggesting that spiritual work should make us better husbands, wives, children, workers, and so on. His approach emphasizes service to others rather than private enlightenment. And even though his material demonstrates the most sincere respect for the historic Jesus, it is the cosmic Christ that emerges as the more significant.

Compassion Is Taught by Experience

Compassion is clearly a wonderful quality, but how do you get it? How do you know when you have it, and how can you keep it? All cultures value this attribute (at least for their own members); therefore, historically they've tried to legislate it into existence. The Sumerians tried, as did the Egyptians, the

Jews, and countless other societies. More recently American civil rights legislation of the 1960s tried to decree compassion. The problem is that true compassion can't be politically ordained. Laws can be written, behavior can be enforced, but no one has found a way to mandate a condition of the heart. Consequently, compassion—the pearl of religion and the flower of culture—can be cultivated only through personal desire. But what fans the flame of this desire? What motivates people to sensitize their hearts to the joys and sufferings of others?

One way to open the heart is to *receive* a compassionate act from someone else. Can you remember a kind word offered to you just when you needed it the most? Few things in life are as powerful. One man shared an experience of his youth that had affected him deeply. He had been intensely involved in a college love affair that eventually began to turn sour. After graduation the girl had gone to a summer job six hours' drive north of the boy's hometown. In a desperate attempt to save the relationship, the boy had borrowed his parents' car, said good-bye to them and his brother, and driven north with high hopes.

Three torturous days later he finally admitted to himself that his attempts were useless—his former love had lost interest in him. Feeling embarrassed and utterly alone, he drove back to his parents' home. He arrived late at night but found his brother awake, watching a late movie. At first the brother was surprised to see him, but almost immediately he understood the situation. A thousand things could have been said, a thousand jokes could have been made, but the brother maintained compassionate silence. He simply invited the traveler to have a soda and watch the movie. The lovesick college boy never forgot this moment. It had filled his heart with gratitude. Driving home, he had felt alone and unloved, yet he found love and companionship in the familiar company of his brother.

You have no doubt had an experience in which you were on the receiving end of someone's compassion. Such moments serve as powerful lessons because their memory can be clearly recalled and they so readily trigger a caring for others. Perhaps it's also the way in which gratitude softens a heart and makes it sensitive to those around us.

Another way of awakening compassion is through suffering.

In the parable that opened this chapter, the widow was overwhelmed with grief. Yet it was this very pain that motivated her to make contact with the sufferings of others. Often our own pain is healed as we commiserate with people who have similar wounds. A recent example of this transformative power surfaced in the wake of the Soviet Union's involvement in the Afghani civil war. In many ways Afghanistan was the Soviets' Vietnam. Many of their young soldiers returned from the fighting with the same physical and emotional trauma that plagued America's young men upon their return from Vietnam. Recently a number of Vietnam veterans felt moved to travel to the Soviet Union and counsel the soldiers who were broken in body and demoralized in spirit. Happily, many of them experienced profound healings of their own as they offered themselves in compassion to their Soviet counterparts.

Meeting others in their suffering is a theme echoed by three Catholic theologians in a powerful book entitled *Compassion: A Reflection on the Christian Life*. This short volume is bound to make any reader uncomfortable, as its authors—Donald McNeill, Douglas Morrison, and Henri Nouwen—challenge us to look beyond general kindness and tenderhearted sympathy and enter compassionately into the pain of others.

These three men, who have tried personally to live what they preach, recognize that the call to authentic compassion meets with inner protest and resistance. In a society that almost worships comfort, why would anyone want consciously to suffer with others?

The authors point out that compassion requires us to be weak with the weak, vulnerable with the vulnerable, and powerless with the powerless—an image reminiscent of Cayce's description of the Christ as one who laughed with those who laughed and wept with those who wept. Yet this element of Cayce's philosophy of life is easily lost in the view of many New Age adherents who are obsessed with personal empowerment and individual development. "Suffering is a messy business," they might say, "and we hope it's all an illusion, anyway."

Nevertheless, we can't have an authentic spirituality unless we deal openly and directly with each other in our brokenness. It's an unavoidable spiritual law for traditional Christians who read the Bible but don't want to hear what these three theologians have to say. And it's just as true for any student of the

Cayce material who may hope for *private* enlightenment. To miss this point is to lose an essential key for creating a positive future. In fact, we may think that compassion is burdensome, an onerous duty if we want to trod the spiritual path. Paradoxically, we find that compassion is a joy and that in the midst of bearing others' pain we are set free of our own.

The Psychology of Compassion

What makes one person compassionate and another person not? Neither kindness nor pain guarantees a transformation of the human heart. Some are raised on love and still think only of themselves. Some suffer all their lives while continuing to have no regard for others.

Even though we may not understand *why* this happens, we can observe *how*. G. I. Gurdjieff, Russian-born teacher of spiritual development and contemporary of Edgar Cayce, contended that there is a psychology of caring about others. According to Gurdjieff, most of us spend our lives spiritually unconscious. We *believe* we know what we're doing and who we are, but in fact we delude ourselves. And as long as we labor under our self-imposed delusions, we react to others in a very self-centered way, often feeling unappreciated and mistreated. Gurdjieff called this pattern "internal considering" because the focus of attention is on oneself.

It's easy to notice this noncompassionate inclination in ourselves. One of its features is the tendency to keep mental records of the times we've been mistreated. Gurdjieff called this thought process "making inner accounts." At the heart of this roadblock to compassion is our preoccupation with being cheated, mistreated, and unappreciated. We fall prey to the whispering of an internal voice: "I'll remember how you slighted me, and you owe me one for that." In such a self-centered condition, there is no room for compassion.

Gurdjieff pointed out that internal considering is the automatic condition of an unconscious life. In other words, it's how most of us behave most of the time. By contrast, *external considering* requires a constant effort to remain spiritually awake. In order to feel and act with compassion, we must develop the capacity to see ourselves in the other person and see the other person in us. Fundamentally it's the experience of oneness applied to human relations.

Of course, all this is easier said than done. We fail so frequently to focus attention on others largely because it seems to require so much of us. Not only are we asked to exercise forgiveness and patience, we must actually experience another's pain. For most of us such a demand is extremely inconvenient, to say the least. We have things to do, places to go, people to see. We hardly have time even to *hear* about someone's suffering, let alone *participate* in it. Compassion can draw us into sacrifices we're not willing to make.

The Power of Compassion

In the early 1940s, as much of the world was ablaze with war, Edgar Cayce was besieged with appeals for readings. An admiring article in a major national magazine and a new biography from a leading publisher had made his name well known. Because of his psychic sensitivity, he could actually feel the anguish in the mailbags filled with requests for readings. Out of compassion, he began giving more readings than his health could endure. By September 1944 he was so exhausted and sick that he could no longer do his work, and by the following January he was dead. Was Cayce's decision to work himself to death a wise one? Who can say? Perhaps his choice was the ultimate statement of his ideal of service. However, might he have served better by conserving his strength? Such decisions are extremely personal, but one thing is sure: When we experience true compassion, we are sometimes faced with such dilemmas.

Compassion is most effective when it's balanced by discernment—enlightened thinking that can see when sacrifice is appropriate and when it's not. A gentle heart needs the companionship of a level head. The daily decisions that require this balance are many, and there are no easy answers. Day by day we create our future by the way we intertwine our thinking, feeling, and willing. These three qualities of the human soul are evolving in each of us. Thinking, feeling, and willing all strive for enlightenment.

Perhaps our cultural emphasis on intellect (thinking) and doing (will) has too often made us forget the power of feeling.

Transformed beyond self-pity, jealousy, and worry, our feeling life can be infused with compassion. It becomes a key to our spiritual destiny because it allows us to "see" things that we cannot see with our normal vision and thinking. Compassion transforms the feeling life of our hearts and allows us to *know* oneness, not merely theorize about it. Where it is absent, there is envy, hatred, fear, and greed. But with compassion comes true happiness and a kind of healing that is inaccessible to the rational mind alone.

EXERCISE

Try to experience consciously the way of knowing that comes through a compassionate heart. This is a two-part exercise, and the results of the second phase depend on success with the first.

Pick one day to focus on the effort. For that twenty-four-hour period, attempt first to disarm "internal considering"—laboring under self-imposed delusions and reacting to others in a very self-centered way, often feeling unappreciated and mistreated. This best way to do this may be to cease making "inner accounts." In other words, stop keeping a mental record of people who "owe you something" because of their insensitivity. Instead, be tolerant. Let things slide off your back. Don't let yourself be offended just for this one day.

As you're successful with the first half of this exercise, watch what you experience next. When your mind isn't busy criticizing other people or keeping records of their offenses, it is free to see them in a new way. Be open to others. Experience with them their pains *and* their joys. Notice the special kind of knowledge that comes to you through a compassionate heart.

Companionship in Joy of Serving and Knowing 165

Transformed and purified by confronting with your feelings will be the negatives that once had such a hold on our spiritual destiny... with the result that we can know the Companionship... Compassion heightens the feeling that our hearts and minds are to begin... attitudes are more... patience about... choices will affirm... is calling indeed... pray and accept... with... compassion comes... purity... the... to the

PRINCIPLE #18

There Is Power in Groups

In the 1940s, as Edgar Cayce entered his final years, he occasionally reflected on all he'd experienced and attempted throughout his life. With the advantage of hindsight, he could see that some of his efforts had ended in defeat. For example, his beloved hospital folded only three years after it opened, and an experiment in higher education—Atlantic University—lasted an even shorter time. However, from the vantage point of his autumn years, Cayce could also see that from the ashes of those defeats rose one of his greatest triumphs: the study group program.

When the hospital closed in 1931, Cayce felt that his life was falling apart. He started to have dreams in which he was on the "other side," giving readings for people who, like himself, had died. His own reading, given soon thereafter to interpret those dreams, warned Cayce's circle of friends that they needed to get him reconnected with a meaningful purpose. Otherwise his soul would follow its calling to where it could better serve. Spurred by this prophecy, several of Cayce's followers formed a small group. At its nucleus was Edgar Cayce, and its purpose was twofold. First, it gave Cayce something meaningful to do; second, it provided a chance to explore the spiritual laws that could help people fulfill their destinies. The group met on a regular basis to receive a reading from Cayce. Each member of the group took time between meetings to apply that information on spiritual laws in daily life as best he or she could.

Later the group wrote a series of lessons on these laws, combining each member's personal experience with the information offered in Cayce's readings. The lessons focused on such principles as cooperation, self-knowledge, spiritual ideals, patience, and faith. The group continued for eleven years, received 130 readings, and compiled the text for twenty-four lessons. By the end of that period Cayce had come to regard the study group project as one of the most important of his life.

Eventually the twenty-four lessons were published in a two-volume series entitled *A Search for God*, and they became the focal point for a worldwide network of study groups. One reading predicted that these volumes would become spiritual guidebooks for thousands of people. That prophecy has been more than fulfilled in the years since Cayce's death. A small group of dedicated individuals rallying around a friend in 1931 accomplished a deed of great significance, creating something that continues to work its magic today for thousands of spiritual seekers.

Small Groups Can Make Big Changes

Turning back the pages of history, we can find many examples of the kind of power demonstrated by Cayce's group of friends. After Gautama Sakyamuni received total enlightenment and became the Buddha around 500 B.C., he gathered around him a small group of monks whose efforts helped create the foundations of a new religion. Five hundred years later Jesus fasted alone for forty days in the wilderness and had a personal encounter with the tempter. Directly after his victory in this spiritual showdown, he reentered society and chose twelve individuals to become members of his inner circle.

Six centuries later a forty-year old member of the Arabian Koraish tribe received revelations as he meditated in a desert cave. His name was Mohammed, and the religion he founded was Islam. In the next two centuries Islam—which, translated, means both "surrender" and "peace"—swept the Middle East and nearly conquered Europe, halted only by the army of Charlemagne. This vast movement began, however, with a small group of five: Mohammed; his wife, Khadija; his young cousin, Ali; a wealthy friend, abu-Bakr; and a freed servant, Zaid.

More recently, the great experiment in democracy that is the United States government was hammered out by a small group of committed individuals. Washington, Jefferson, Adams, Franklin, and their colleagues assembled a government stable and flexible enough to weather the drastic changes of the last two hundred years.

Given all these historical examples, it's easy to agree with anthropologist Margaret Mead on this point: "Never doubt that a small group of thoughtful, committed citizens can change the world; indeed, it's the only thing that ever has."

Why Does a Group Have Power?

What is it about small groups? Why do they seem to generate so much force? Probably the best way to answer this question is to examine it from the perspective of physics. Everyone knows about the power of a magnet, but from where does that power come? Although the physical principles involved are still rather mysterious, we do know that magnetism is the result of an *alignment* of the electrical polarities of each atom. In an unmagnetized piece of iron, the atomic electrical charges are arranged randomly, with positive and negative poles scattered in all possible directions. However, once those electrical polarities line up in the same orientation, the magnetic properties immediately appear.

In the same way, when small groups of individuals align their purposes along a common ideal, they generate a field of power. The strength of this field is in direct proportion to the sincerity of each member. True alignment isn't achieved just through lip service: a real commitment is necessary.

In June 1940, sixty-four people gathered around Edgar Cayce as he gave a reading on the world situation. Many questions were asked about the future developments of the war that was already raging in Europe and the Orient. That reading boldly asserted that if those sixty-four individuals combined their prayers for peace and committed their lives to the same ideal, they could significantly influence the course of the war. The reading stressed the importance of each individual's sincerity. A small group can be very effective *if* the purposes and ideals of the members are truly in accord. If there is dissension, however, the power dissipates.

This principle is known as the law of synergy; in other words, the whole is more than the sum of its parts. Group members who cooperatively blend their intentions, purposes, and actions can create something far more influential than might be expected logically. It is as if something were added to the total of human efforts, something that comes from a higher source. As noted earlier, perhaps the best analogy for demonstrating this spiritual law can be found in music. When you play three notes on a piano that are in harmony with each other, you create a special blend. The sensitive ear can still discern the individual notes, but added to them is the sound of a *chord*.

What Is the Nature of Group Power?

The alignment of purpose that can be achieved in a group pools the energies of each member. Just as it is easier to move a piano with four people than with only one, the energies of mind and will are intensified when applied cooperatively. Anyone who's been involved in a "think tank" situation knows the kind of mental creativity that can be generated by a small group tossing ideas back and forth. One person's insight triggers that of another. Creativity is bound to be much more intense with this cooperative approach than would be the case if group members went into separate rooms and later simply compiled their individual thoughts.

A high school dramatics coach told the story of how he discovered the group effect during a difficult rehearsal for his school's spring production. As the director, he had accepted the responsibility of selecting the play and had chosen an English farce with complicated blocking (stage movements by the actors and actresses). There were many entrances and exits that needed to be coordinated to accent the humor of the play.

The coach scheduled a special rehearsal in which to practice this blocking with his cast of students. Unfortunately, none of it seemed successful. His plans went awry. The blocking that had been worked out so well in his imagination created all sorts of problems when actually applied onstage. Finally he called the cast together and apologized. He suggested that they end the rehearsal early and that he would try to overhaul his plans for the stage movements.

To his surprise and delight, the students wanted to stay and work out the blocking together. Encouraged by their enthusiasm, the drama coach forged ahead. However, this time, instead of moving the characters around as if they were puppets, he involved them in the creative process. Soon everything was falling into place. By the end of that rehearsal everyone felt the special energy that accompanies successful, creative collaboration. It came as no surprise to the director that the play eventually proved to be a big hit.

In addition to an increase of mental power, groups also create a heightened power of will. This is illustrated by one fundamental part of Cayce's study group program: the weekly discipline. The idea of using personal will to *apply* what is being studied goes back to the 1930s, when Cayce gave readings to the original group on each of the twenty-four spiritual laws. Occasionally, when the members met for a reading, the psychic discourse would be extremely brief. If the members of the group had failed to put into practice what had been presented in the last reading, no further information was offered. In other words, spiritual growth comes from doing something with these ideas, not just hearing them or talking about them.

In the thousands of groups that have since organized around Cayce's *A Search for God* books, the weekly discipline is a pivotal element. At each meeting the group members decide on a way to apply in daily life what they've been studying. Then, at the next meeting (usually a week later), they share their experiences and reflections based on that personal experiment.

For example, one passage from *A Search for God* refers to the replacement of negative thoughts with positive ones and encourages us to think and speak kindly of everyone. At the end of a meeting one group might choose this idea to apply as a weekly discipline. No doubt we can all appreciate the difficulty of speaking *and* thinking kindly of everyone for even a day, let alone a whole week. However, the fact that an entire group is cooperating in the effort creates a *collective will* that makes the discipline more achievable. The group's intention and commitment enable each individual member to draw upon his or her inner resources for success with the task.

Probably the most impressive example of group will is Alcoholics Anonymous (AA). By banding together with other sufferers, an alcoholic can benefit from the collective will the group generates. AA has proved so successful that its basic model has been applied to many other addictions, including drugs, food, and money. In every case the power of the group helps the individual strengthen his or her personal will.

The Dark Side of Group Power

We hear a great deal these days about cults. Most people probably have some idea which groups are or are not cultish. The dictionary refers to a cult in broad terms as any "formally established devotional group," which could conceivably include the various forms of organized religion as well. However, the word *cult* has recently acquired a more specific meaning, one in which the power of the group is more often applied selfishly and destructively.

According to this connotation, then, what turns a group into a cult? How might we describe "cult consciousness"? The most recognizable feature is an exaggeration of the alignment principle mentioned earlier. You'll recall that the power of a group can be generated by an alignment of the purposes and ideals held by each member, just as the electrical polarities of magnetized iron point in the same direction. The Cayce readings affirm that a unison of purpose produces group power. However, in a cult this unison is extended beyond purposes and ideals; the members are required to align their very thinking according to the cult's dogma. Cults generally have a charismatic leader or a body of "revealed truth" that is accorded absolute authority. To question this authority constitutes heresy, and such an offense is usually punished. Sometimes the punishment is physical, but most often offenders are censured psychologically through forced penances or a period of shunning by other cult members.

In contrast, a *healthy* group encourages individuality even as it seeks unison. The Cayce readings address this careful balance by affirming that group members can share a common *ideal* while at the same time holding very different *ideas*.

In the opinion of some people, Cayce's psychic information is an example of the "revealed truth" around which a cult forms. However, the readings deny such status by inviting analytic discussion and encouraging a critical examination by both individuals and research organizations. The material should be "cussed and discussed," as one reading put it.

A second key feature of cult consciousness is the tendency

to avoid outside contact. Cult members sometimes enter mainstream society to ask for donations or proselytize for the movement, but they are discouraged from any kind of intellectual or emotional interaction with outsiders. In fact, a cult generates solidarity by instilling in its members fear and distrust of the outside world. Leaders may teach, *"They* are full of wickedness. *They* are out to get us. *They* are responsible for all your problems."* The cult, of course, promises to provide for the members' every need: "*We* understand you. *We* can protect you. *We* will take care of you." By generating an atmosphere of paranoia, the cult assures the allegiance of its members.

Healthy groups, by contrast, encourage and welcome interaction with society at large. Cayce's readings consistently urged people to get involved with a wide variety of groups, including churches and civic organizations.

Power for What?

Like all forms of power, the influence of groups can be channeled either constructively or destructively. Adolf Hitler, the Buddha, Jesus, Charles Manson, and Mohammed all employed the power of the small group to initiate their respective visions. But their results were quite different. Groups, like the individual, have the power to create either crimes or miracles.

The Cayce readings also emphasized the group's power *to heal*. In 1931, shortly after the initiation of the study group project, Cayce dreamed that certain members of the group had gathered for another special project: the study of healing prayer. Prompted by his dream, Cayce actually formed a "group within a group," which continued for thirteen years and received sixty-five readings on the healing power of prayer. Its final reading was given only months before Cayce's death. Since then that original group has evolved into an ongoing assembly of about two dozen people called the Glad Helpers Healing Prayer Group, which continues to meet weekly, offering itself as a channel of healing prayer for anyone who asks.

The readings stress a second application of group power: self-transformation. The very purpose of the Cayce small group program is to raise human nature to its full spiritual potential. Doing that requires honest self-examination and persistent discipline. Left on our own, we may find this kind of work difficult. However, the dynamics of group consciousness—the collective mind and will created by a group sharing a common purpose—can make the difference.

Finally, by transforming ourselves, we transform the world. One member of a Cayce *A Search for God* study group humorously commented, "After working in the group for a few months, I was surprised to discover that people in my life seemed much nicer." Of course, implied in this comment was that *she* had changed and that with her new attitudes she perceived the world in a better way.

We've already observed how small groups of committed individuals have had a profound impact on history. Examples such as Buddha, Jesus, and Mohammed are but the classics; history offers cases of countless groups that have labored quietly through the centuries to improve conditions in the world. Indeed, this seems to be the way we humans work best.

Not only do we find a special power for healing and self-transformation through groups, we *need* them because we need each other. This point comes through clearly in the story about a man who went to his pastor and announced that he wouldn't be coming to church anymore since he'd decided that God could be worshiped just as easily at home or on the golf course. The pastor listened patiently and then walked over to a blazing fire, scooped out one ember, and placed it on the hearth. After just a few moments the ember was cold. The man stood up and said, "I'll see you in church."

EXERCISE

Take note of the groups in which you already participate: at home, at work, in your community. Select one in which you feel there is an especially strong potential for healing and self-transformation (for yourself *and* for the other members of the group). Of course, not every group's overt purpose for existence is healing or self-transformation, but these features can still be present if some of the group members act on the possibility.

Make a recommitment to this one particular group effort. What can you do to be more authentically present to this group, to bring your full self to the group's life and activities? And then, in the days ahead, try to act more consciously as a member of that team.

PART FOUR

Strategies for a New Life

PRINCIPLE #19

Take the Initiative: It's Best to Be Doing Something

During a troubled romance, a young woman confided to her friend, "I have so much anxiety about deciding what's the right thing to do that I end up doing nothing."

This is a trap we all may fall into from time to time. Feeling uncertain or discouraged, we may silently ask the universe to give us a boost, a jump start, a leg up. We may promise that if something will just get us started in the right direction, we'll take it from there:

> I'd like to patch up the relationship with my neighbor, who's been mad at me for months, but I don't know what to say first.

> I want to save money for my retirement, but I don't know what sort of investment is really best.

Often the biggest challenge is taking the first step. The task can occasionally seem so daunting that we trick ourselves into believing we've already done it when we actually haven't. This type of self-deception is analogous to the story about a boy who wanted to learn how to ride a bicycle and enlisted the help of his older brother. The brother put him on the seat and pushed the bike, then ran alongside. When enough speed was built up, the brother turned the bike loose and the young boy steered the bike until it ran out of steam and fell over. The young boy, however, was very excited. He told all his friends that he had learned to ride a bicycle. It never occurred to him that he couldn't even keep it going, let alone get it started in the first place. He had ridden the contraption by himself, and that was enough. With childish self-deception, he missed the point: Until he has learned how to get the bicycle started on his own, he hasn't actually mastered the task.

Don't we often feel the same way about some of our own accomplishments? If life is carrying us along relatively well, we smile contentedly and say, "I'm doing a pretty good job." Yet to accept the invitation to become cocreators with God, we need to learn more than just how to navigate the currents of life. We need to learn how to build up some steam and forge ahead. This takes initiative, the ability to take that first step. We need to know how to get the bicycle started as well as how to ride it.

What Is Initiative?

The word *initiative* comes from a Latin root that also gives us the word *initiate*. In the mystery religions of Greece and Egypt, those who entered into the secret teachings were called initiates. They had taken the first steps toward spiritual enlightenment. Their experiences were designed to change them mentally and spiritually. Through the disciplines of diet, exercise, concentration, and meditation, these initiates would face the deepest parts of their inner consciousness. Eventually they would come face to face with the ultimate mysteries of the spiritual realms and return to the world of daylight with knowledge and wisdom born of their spiritual initiation. This was the actual purpose of the mystery religions: to provide the initiate with spiritual insights that only direct experience could bring.

Today we are also called to achieve spiritual growth. We can be modern-day initiates. The process may include some of the ancient techniques, such as meditation, but initiation also has a distinctly contemporary meaning—that of "taking initiatives" in the world around us. That means *doing something,* courageously taking the first step.

Sometimes these initial steps may seem formidable. In countless myths and folktales spiritual initiation is dramatized in the form of seemingly impossible tasks that the hero or heroine must perform. The reward comes only if the protagonist first *does* something. Perhaps one of the best-known examples of this aspect of spiritual initiation is found in the Greek story of the twelve labors of Heracles (or Hercules, in the Roman version).

Consumed with grief over having committed a crime of passion, Heracles went to the oracle at Delphi and asked how he might atone for his action. The oracle told him that the breakthrough and inner release he sought had to be preceded by actions in the world. He was required to offer himself in service to his cousin, Eurystheus, king of Mycenae. The king gave Heracles twelve labors, each of which was, of course, a superhuman task. Some of the labors involved battling monsters; some were hunting exploits. Perhaps the best known of the twelve was his fifth assignment: to clean the Augean stables—which housed thousands of cattle and hadn't been cleaned in years—in one day! Heracles succeeded at this task, as well as at all the others, and at the end of his long life of adventures he was admitted into the company of the gods and married the divine cupbearer, Hebe.

Inner spiritual growth is *dependent* on outer physical effort. Heracles couldn't just wait around hoping to be forgiven for his misdeed; he had to get the ball rolling by doing something. The purpose of this and every similar myth is to help us understand our own story. Sometimes we, too, feel burdened with problems beyond our understanding. We may also feel occasionally that the tasks before us are as vast and disagreeable as cleaning the Augean stables. But there is comfort in this promise: Life changes for us when we start doing something—as soon as we take the initiative with the challenges at hand.

We Learn by Doing

Thousands of people came to Edgar Cayce for advice. Sometimes their problems were mundane or trivial; often they sought help with matters of life and death. It's remarkable how frequently he advised simply, "Get busy" or "Do something" or "Begin now." Often accompanying these admonitions was the promise that further guidance would unfold naturally as one actually began to do something about the concern.

G. I. Gurdjieff illustrated this principle of cosmic law with the use of a parable. It has been retold by many of his students, such as Maurice Nicoll in *Psychological Commentaries on the Teachings of Gurdjieff and Ouspensky*. Imagine you see before you a carriage, a horse, and a driver. The carriage represents the physical body, the horse depicts the power of the emotions, and the driver corresponds to the intellect. However, all is not well in this scene. Symbolizing the usual inner condition of a typical human being, the driver is intoxicated and has abandoned or forgotten his duties. He is in the public bar, wasting his money and drunkenly assuming what he thinks is the identity of his master. Outside, his horse is unfed and sickly, and the carriage is falling into disrepair. Before the master can come and take charge of the situation, the driver must wake up, put the horse and carriage in order, and again take his post on the driver's box.

The master of the carriage symbolizes your true identity. Carl Jung would call it your "Self," and the Cayce readings would call it your "individuality." The carriage master represents the part of you that knows where it's going and how to get there, the part that knows your destiny.

The first part of the parable describes the importance of getting your intellectual, emotional, and physical bodies in good working condition before expecting your "master" to come into the carriage. But there is a further element of the parable, one with tremendous significance. Even after the master has entered the carriage, he or she will not give instructions until the driver has taken his best guess on the appropriate direction and *started the carriage moving*. Once that initiative has been taken, it's the driver's job to listen intently for instructions from the master.

Gurdjieff's story effectively describes a universe that is responsive to our efforts. As we take the first step and do our best with what we know how to do, opportunities will open up to us naturally, through the action of spiritual law.

Do What You Can; More Will Be Given

We don't have to look far to find evidence for and confirmation of the reliability of this process. For example, an actress has told about her tough experiences trying to find work in the crucible of New York City. Almost daily she obtained the major trade papers listing the auditions being held that week and noted the ones that looked promising. She organized her days carefully so that she would make every audition, as well as visit any number of agents in the city.

This was exhausting work and usually was not very satisfying. Often at the end of the week she had nothing to show for her efforts. Every door she had knocked on remained closed. However, over time she noticed that when she conscientiously kept up her rounds, an opportunity for work would present itself, frequently in an unexpected way. Often the door of opportunity was not even one on which she had knocked. She came to believe that her very effort was in some way inviting these opportunities into her life even when she could see no clear relationship between the doors she knocked on and the ones that opened.

Another story involves a man facing a career crisis. He had worked himself into a job that he enjoyed but in which he saw no discernible long-term future. He was confronted with the common problem of choosing a new vocational direction and initiating the change. Everyone who has faced this sort of crossroads knows the tremendous strain it can impose and the sense of inertia that often comes with it. This man was in just that situation, feeling almost paralyzed, incapable of action. However, a little push gave him the opportunity to get the ball rolling. A friend of his had a dream that appeared to be telepathic and indicated a possible career direction. Within a few days of hearing this dream, the man had taken some steps, setting up three separate interviews with career professionals who could provide perspectives on a possible move. From these initiatives, the man not only got vital insights and information but also found substantial help in effecting this difficult midlife change.

The Cayce readings focused repeatedly on the importance of doing something. Take, for example, Cayce's novel perspective on Jesus' first recorded miracle: the turning of water into wine. As this miracle is described in the Gospel of John, Jesus instructed the servants of the house to pour enough water to fill six stone jugs. Then, when the fluid was drawn out, it was discovered to be wine. The usual view of this miracle is that the water changed astoundingly into wine as it sat in the containers. But Cayce, in commenting on this miracle, stressed the important element of taking the initiative. It was the deed of *pouring* the water that transformed it into wine. Thus, even in miracles action is necessary.

But What If I Do the Wrong Thing?

In all these stories the higher forces seem to respond to sincere efforts on our part. Even when we're not sure what direction is best, we're encouraged to make a choice and take a step. If the direction is inappropriate to our best interests, the universe will give us the necessary feedback, but we have to move if we want God to respond. Even a wrong move can provide vital instruction. As Carl Jung once wrote, "Error is just as important a condition of life's progress as truth."

In 1943 a thirty-four-year-old woman from New York City wrote Edgar Cayce and asked for a reading on her past lives. Along with her request she included a list of questions, many of which focused on finding her soul's purpose as well as trying to understand her current life situation. She hoped that the reading would help her find true love, reconcile herself to a major accident, and launch a meaningful career. But many of her questions centered on one concern: whether her soul had been progressing or regressing during the last few lifetimes. When that question was finally asked during the reading, the unconscious Cayce responded that there is always progress whether one is going forward or backward; the key is to accomplish *some* kind of movement.

Clearly this woman needed to hear about the importance of action. Apparently she suffered from an ailment that besets many of us these days: "the paralysis of analysis." We can devote so much time and energy to analyzing a situation that we never get around to doing anything about it. We can get so proficient at considering all sides of an issue that we wind up offering what astrologers might call the Libran prayer: "Lord, help me to be more decisive . . . but on the other hand, what do You think?"

The consequences of inaction may perhaps best be illustrated by the character of Hamlet in Shakespeare's famous tragedy. Here is a young man who is called on to avenge the murder of his father. He plots and he schemes, he muses and he raves . . . but he does not act. When the play finally ends, eight people are dead: the guilty party, many innocent people, and Hamlet himself, a victim of his own inertia.

By contrast, even the most glaring errors of activity ultimately can lead to major accomplishments. One of the most dramatic examples is Saint Paul's conversion as recorded in the Acts of the Apostles. Paul's determined persecution of the new Christian religion set him on the road to Damascus. On that fateful day, as he was blinded by the light, his sincere—though misguided—initiative was redirected toward a higher purpose.

Drastic errors may, of course, be avoided if we can cultivate the fine art of ongoing examination and assessment. The point is to take the first step and then evaluate the results carefully before pushing on. The following illustrates how events can otherwise go wrong.

Upon returning from a Peace Corps stint in the Philippines, a volunteer told the story of the "ceiling gecko." Some well-meaning volunteers were working in a group of villages that were infested with cockroaches. This condition seemed deplorable to the Americans, and they immediately set about using pesticides to eradicate offensive insects from each and every dwelling in all the neighboring villages. Eventually they succeeded and felt very gratified about their accomplishment. Unfortunately, before long they noticed new and even worse invaders—rats! Struggling to overcome this disturbing turn of events, they began to understand more fully the local ecology. The cockroaches had been a prime food for the ceiling gecko, a lizard that lived in the ceilings and walls of the local dwellings. The gecko had always been considered good luck by the local inhabitants, and the volunteers finally realized why: the ceiling geckos had been keeping away the rats. Without the cockroaches there were *no* geckos, and without the geckos there were lots of rats.

The Peace Corps volunteers took the initiative all right, but it made things worse. What went wrong? Aren't conditions supposed to get better when we do *something* rather than nothing at all? Not necessarily. Every initiative must be followed by a period of reflection. Rather than *test* their action in a small-scale way, the volunteers sprayed pesticides throughout the region. Their intentions were good, but a more balanced approach would have been better.

At the heart of this concept of "right action" is a simple three-step formula:

1. Don't get stuck with inertia, waiting for something to happen. Take an initial small step of action.
2. Observe the results. Does your initiative seem to have worked as you hoped—thereby encouraging you to continue? Or are there signs that a different course of action is needed?
3. Keep applying, perhaps adjusting to, the feedback you've received. Continue to act with the best information you have at your disposal.

EXERCISE

Pick an area of your life where you feel stuck or stagnant. How do you experience that inertia? What emotions are associated with it? Fear? Confusion? Frustration?

Get the ball rolling with some kind of initiative, no matter how small. Make a firm resolution to take some little step, then do it. Be at peace with the assurance that until you've had a chance to evaluate the results, you're making no commitment bigger than that one initial step.

Give If You Want to Receive: Only What You Give Away Do You Own

Your future is only as real as the resources you have to create it. A great plan isn't worth much unless you have the time, energy, and money to make it happen. Sometimes the difference between a dreamy idealist and a successful person is simply the possession of material assets.

It's not surprising that Edgar Cayce was often asked questions concerning money and other physical resources. People usually came to him with the desire to build a better future, but often they knew that practical matters like money stood in their way. Many of the readings were given during the Depression years, when such concerns were even more widespread. During the 1930s individuals saw their fortunes wiped out; life savings sometimes disappeared overnight. Some of these people believed that the advice from Cayce was their last hope for re-creating prosperous times.

For example, in 1937 a fifty-five-year-old woman who was grappling with a financial crisis asked in her reading for counsel toward achieving monetary security. Perhaps she was expecting recommendations on investment strategies or lucrative career options. Instead Cayce gave her a spiritual perspective on abundance. He reminded her of a biblical principle: "Every wild animal of the forest is mine, the cattle on a thousand hills" (Psalm 50). In other words, every type of material resource ultimately belongs to God. Finally, Cayce encouraged the woman to follow a universal principle: What you give, you have; as you give more, the fruits will come.

In today's sophisticated business climate, this suggestion sounds admirable but naive. Anyone with commercial savvy knows that you don't get rich by giving anything away. The assertion that material security can be achieved through the act of giving is likely to fall on deaf ears. In the mind-set of mainstream culture, there isn't enough material to go around, so "you'd better get yours while you can."

That way of thinking may make sense from a logical point of view, but what are the results of such a philosophy when put into practice? The evidence suggests that in the long run hoarding leads to shortage and greed fails to achieve happiness. As radical—even as illogical—as it may sound, the secret to abundance may actually lie in the attitude and act of sharing. Giving makes sense in light of the principle of oneness. Because we are deeply unified and connected with other human beings, we are essentially giving to ourselves when we share. Because we are one with God, we can acknowledge the spiritual dimension of life as the ultimate source of any material asset.

The Law of Material Supply

A set of reliable rules controls the flow of physical resources such as money, food, and energy. Just as governmental laws direct the exchange of finances, a spiritual law regulates all forms of material supply. The law is simple but not easy to apply. (Some of its components have been described in earlier chapters.) First is the formula "Spirit is the life, mind is the builder, and the physical is the result." Thus, the spirit is the source of *all* things, including money and material possessions, and the spiritual process of manifesting these resources begins in the mind.

We need to be careful, however, at this point. Spiritual law as it relates to material supply has often been distorted by those looking for shortcuts to prosperity or excuses for their greed. "Mind is the builder" shouldn't imply that in order to possess a million dollars all one needs to do is concentrate long and hard enough on mental images of wealth. Many New Age proponents of "prosperity consciousness" recommend exactly this practice, but in fact the mind helps create material resources in quite a different way. It's the purpose toward which you intend to apply the resources that needs your attention and concentration, a purpose that extends beyond mere self-interest. If your mind is focused on what you're doing and why, your needs will be met.

Giving Opens the Door

Merely knowing and understanding the law doesn't make it work for you. You still need to *do* things to create the flow of material resources. As you give what you have, you create the space for new blessings to flow your way. The physical world often illustrates this principle; electricity is one excellent example. In order for electrical current to flow, lighting our lamps and running our dishwashers, a completed circuit is needed. If at any point the electrons are not allowed to pass, the electrical current ceases. The same is true in the flow of material resources. By passing on some of the bounty you receive, you encourage its circulation. Giving prepares the way for receiving.

However, it's a mistake to regard this spiritual law as something to manipulate in a clever or self-serving way. Take the story of Robert, who could never find a parking space when he wanted one. This difficulty irritated him more than almost anything else. His problem became the topic one night in a discussion group that gathered weekly to study spiritual law. This particular evening Robert and the others were focusing on the laws that govern material supply, specifically the concept that giving is the key to receiving. The next day Robert decided to test the theory and "prime the pump" of his own abundance by supplying quarters to expired parking meters, thereby giving to the anonymous owners of the parked cars. For a while afterward he seemed to find a parking space whenever he wanted one. He happily reported to his group that he now fully understood the law of supply. But did he?

Robert had grasped the essentials of the law of abundance but had applied it only in a very narrow and manipulative way. First, it was as if he had tried to forge a contractual arrangement with higher spiritual sources: I'll feed overdue parking meters with quarters, and you feed me with convenient parking spots. Robert's second mistake was to attempt selfish manipulation of the law. If he was giving only because he wanted to receive, then he missed the essence of the principle. Authentic giving carries with it a genuine desire to share with another. What counts is an attitude of generosity, helpfulness, and compassion. If these qualities are absent, no amount of clever manipulation will force material supply to flow into your life. As in Robert's case, it may appear to work—for a time—but the effects are not long-lasting.

Needs and Wants

In the Middle Ages religion promised a life of bliss and fulfillment in the hereafter. Life on earth might be destitute and oppressive, but that was advantageous because it helped liberate souls from the entrapment of the flesh. Poverty was a virtue equal to chastity and obedience. However, the Reformation changed those attitudes, and eventually what developed was the Protestant work ethic, which affirmed that God can reward the faithful even in *this* life.

Today some people believe that God will give you whatever you want if you just know how to ask. Certain religious books provide instructions on how to pray yourself into wealth. New Age lessons abound on the use of crystals and subliminal tapes to draw riches to you. In short, whereas poverty was once regarded as a virtue, the modern world is full of individuals who believe that the result of virtuous living is wealth and riches. In some respects these "spiritual systems" are just new masks for old-fashioned greed.

The Cayce readings recommend a middle ground—a point of balance between these two extremes—that may be arrived at by distinguishing needs from wants. Most of us, for example, *want* a great deal more than we *need*. In fact, we can know our real needs only once we determine the work and purpose to which we're committed.

In 1936 a middle-aged woman sought help from Edgar Cayce. She had been suffering such anxiety over her financial situation that it was interfering with her physical health. In addition to some medical advice, her reading encouraged her to focus more attention on the work the Lord had given her to do: caring for those around her. By giving herself to this work rather than to her fears, she could improve her financial situation. Included in Cayce's counsel was the promise that neither she nor her children would "beg bread" if she was truly seeking to "be a channel of His love."

Cayce's strategy for curing financial ills is a far cry from a formula promising untold riches. Those who follow his philosophy for abundance can expect that their needs will be met as long as they are honestly concerned for the well-being of others. How does one follow that philosophy? How can you cooperate responsibly with the law of supply so that it will assist you in meeting your material needs? Following are six suggestions that can help you apply this law in a positive, creative way.

How to Work with the Law of Supply

1. Clarify Your Purpose

Get clear on your purpose for wanting certain material resources. There's nothing wrong with desiring a home, a car, or a bigger paycheck, but it's helpful to see in those desires some purpose or reason that extends beyond your own gratification. Can you see more possessions or large supplies of money as things that in turn allow you to help others more effectively?

Try this approach to financial planning. First, clarify what you believe to be your purpose as a soul for this lifetime. What is your mission, your creative service to the world? Second, determine what material resources you'll need to be successful in that work. Then set goals and strategies for cocreating with God the material assets you'll require in the future. The next five steps will suggest how to do that.

2. Look for Lessons in Your Areas of Shortage

The Creator knows your needs, in many instances better than you know them yourself. Unquestionably, you require a certain amount of material possessions, but you may also need experiences that lead you to a deeper understanding about yourself and others. Sometimes these lessons may involve periods of lack that test your fortitude, faith, or appreciation. Or your spiritual growth may necessitate achieving a greater sensitivity to the needs of others.

This truth was made vividly plain to a middle-class woman who suddenly lost everything. Her husband got laid off from his factory job. Within a month she found herself out of work as well. For a while unemployment benefits helped them make ends meet. When that ran out, they had to use their meager savings. Eventually that was drained, and they had nothing else. Even their home was taken from them, and they were forced into the surreal experience of living on the street. At last they turned for shelter and food to local charity groups, fully immersed in a social situation that they had never thought twice about before. It was humiliating, but it was also enlightening, as they became acquainted with many others who shared their predicament. The woman swore that if they ever got out of that nightmare, she would not forget the others who suffered the fate of homelessness.

Eventually events turned around for this couple. The husband found work in a new city. She, too, found a job, and their economic situation slowly improved. Within two years they were able to make a down payment on a house and reenter the mainstream of middle America. Through an acquaintance, the woman heard about a charity group headed by private citizens. She telephoned and said, ''I want to deliver a truckload of food to wherever it's needed.''

She made good on that offer and continued to donate her time and money to the cause of the homeless and hungry. By her own admission, the temporary period of shortage had awakened in her a sensitivity for the poverty-stricken. She had made good use of the difficult times. By allowing shortages to teach her an important lesson in compassion, she was able to reestablish a harmonious relationship with the law of supply.

3. Learn to Be Grateful for What You Do Have

Too often in our quest for more and better we overlook the abundance we already have. Our compulsion to acquire more can distort our perception. By ignoring the blessings at hand, we risk losing the abundance we already have. Who among us isn't already blessed? Often it is those in the worst long-term financial circumstances who are the quickest to remember assets such as friendship, love, and health. An appreciation for the resources at hand is a crucial step toward getting in sync with the law of supply.

4. Give What You Can

Giving generously doesn't necessarily mean parting with huge sums of money. It means giving what you can freely and without reservation. It's a lame excuse to promise, "I'll give when I have a little more to offer." Cayce warned several individuals that if they weren't willing to give *something* even when they were hard up, they wouldn't give later if they had a million dollars. The point is to start sharing. If you can't give ten percent right now, that's all right. But what about giving one percent or even one-tenth of one percent?

Remember, money and possessions aren't the only items you have to give. You can also devote time, talent, or energy. Today, "How much time will it take?" is often asked before "How much will it cost?" Time and talents can also be valuable. So take stock of your skills. Which ones can you contribute occasionally for the benefit of someone else?

In addition, keep in mind that the giving of your possessions may not imply literal loss of ownership. It may mean simply offering the *use* of what you have to help another. For example, you might offer your car to carry food to shut-ins. You might offer your home as a weekly meeting place for some group that shares your spiritual commitments. Something important happens when you contribute the use of your possessions without necessarily relinquishing title to them. The loosening of attachments—the diminishing of the objects' possession *of you*—makes room for additional resources to flow into your life.

5. Expect and Accept the Good That Comes to You

"If you give blessings, you will receive blessings." That's a spiritual law. However, this law is not specific about *when* you will receive the blessing or in what *form* it will come. Stay alert and be expectant. Remember that the return won't always take the form of money or possessions. But it will be whatever your soul most needs for its next step toward enlightenment.

The American short-story writer William Sydney Porter, better known by his pen name, O. Henry, understood this principle. He left us a beautiful illustration of how giving can generate rewards that are more valuable than any amount of material gain. His story "Gift of the Magi" focuses on a newly married couple, deeply in love although desperately poor. Of their meager possessions, they deem only two to be of exceptional value. One is the husband's heirloom watch; the other is the wife's cascade of beautiful hair. Christmas is coming, and each is anguishing silently over the inability to get the other a present. Each has the perfect gift in mind for the other: The wife has found a pocket chain for her beloved's treasured watch; her husband has his eye on a set of hair combs that would perfectly decorate her gorgeous hair. But, alas, there is no money for these gifts, and the impending holiday is contemplated with growing despair.

Secretively, they each hit upon an idea to provide the other with the elusive gift, although both plans require a painful sacrifice. The husband pawns his watch to pay for the combs, and the wife cuts and sells her hair to pay for the chain. The end of the story provokes both tears and laughter. It's true that both gifts are rendered useless because of the respective sacrifices. However, the love and devotion each had shown the other in pursuit of a Christmas present fill their hearts to overflowing and bless their day beyond measure.

The benefits that return to us through our giving, as we've noted before, may not always be material. Sometimes they are of much greater value.

6. Giving and Receiving Build Community

Community develops naturally out of giving and receiving, and through this exchange relations are born and nurtured. In a sense, we might say that civilization itself is based on this mutual interaction. How we decide to address the question of give-and-take shapes the quality of life in our world. One of the best illustrations of this principle is the parable of a man who was given the opportunity by an angel to visit heaven and hell.

They visited hell first and saw a depressing scene. A vast banquet table was filled with every imaginable kind of food. Seated around the table were the citizens of hell. But the table was overly large, and the food could be reached only with long utensils strapped to the patrons' wrists. Although they could reach the food, the length of the utensils made it impossible to get the food to their own mouths. This left the residents of hell hungry and tormented with frustration.

Eager to leave the scene, the man asked to visit heaven. He was astounded to discover that heaven had exactly the same setting, with one striking contrast. The residents of heaven were all happy, well fed, and sociable. Mystified, the man asked his angel how this could be, and he was instructed simply to watch more closely. He then discovered the fundamental difference between heaven and hell: Instead of struggling in vain to feed themselves, the souls in heaven effortlessly fed one another.

We can create a little piece of heaven right where we are by giving in love to others and accepting gratefully the bounty that returns.

EXERCISE

The flow of abundance can get blocked at any one of six steps:

1. *Clarify your purpose.* Have a clear sense of what your life is about and what you value most.
2. *Look for lessons in your areas of shortage.* The aspects of your life where there is a lack exist to teach you something.
3. *Learn to be grateful for what you do have.* Move beyond distorted perceptions and see clearly the parts of your life where you *are* greatly blessed.
4. *Give what you can.* By joyfully and freely giving, you redefine yourself as someone whose life is abundant.
5. *Expect and accept the good that comes to you.* Be alert to the necessary resources in whatever form they may come—expected or unexpected.
6. *Giving and receiving build community.* Be open to building or reinforcing interpersonal relations based on mutual care.

Look over the list of six points. Which one of them seems weakest in your life? That is, which one is most in need of further application? Make a personal commitment to do something about it and follow through with your resolution.

Why Worry When You Can Pray?

A popular song by Bobby McFerrin repeats over and over again, "Don't worry, be happy." That's good advice for coping with today's world. We have lots to worry about—so much, in fact, that it's hard to stop. Sometimes we may wake up feeling worried and have to sift through all the issues we're juggling with in order to determine which one is worrying us the most! "Am I worried about paying the bills? About getting that project done on time? About my health? Nuclear war? The ozone layer?"

When you're in the midst of it, worrying seems absolutely logical. How could anyone *not* worry about issues as pressing and precarious as yours? But has anyone ever discovered that worrying improves a situation one whit? Has it ever gotten the bills paid or the project finished? Has it ever improved your health? Of course not. On the contrary, the one thing it *can* do, and do very effectively, is make you sick.

In 1934 a twelve-year-old girl got a Cayce reading to check on her healing progress. She and her parents had been working with Cayce for some time in treating her cancer. In the reading her parents asked, "Are the poisons now being eliminated from her system?" Cayce responded in the affirmative, but with one exception. When the girl allowed herself to worry, her healing was undermined. Worrying caused the poisons to *accumulate* quickly.

Worry is a major factor in many physical ailments. Cayce warned a woman of fifty-five that it was harder on her body than lack of rest. Another woman inquired why she was losing so much weight, and Cayce told her that most of it was due to worrying.

Generally, worry leaves both the body and the mind unfit for handling whatever tasks need to be done. Ironically, it actually prevents us from dealing effectively with what we're worried about. Why, then, do we worry? How is it that worry can so easily possess us?

Tracing the Roots of Worry

It was four-fifteen in the morning. John was tossing and turning in his bed. He knew he was annoying his wife, so he got up and moved into the living room. Wide awake but still in an altered predawn consciousness, he pondered on what could be bothering him. At first the answer was simple: He was worried. The family was facing a major move, many details were uncertain. He was going back to school, and this involved relocating: selling their house, moving all their possessions, buying a new home. How were they going to pay for it? What if they couldn't find a new home in time? Was the whole idea a mistake? So many questions and so few answers. No wonder he couldn't sleep. Worry possessed him.

However, John didn't stop there, because he wanted to see clearly what was going on in his mind. He knew he was worried, but he pressed on in his reflection, asking himself, What is *causing* the worry? Life itself is always a matter of making changes and facing uncertainty; why do I allow these natural experiences to twist my thoughts and emotions?

In the rare clarity that sometimes comes in twilight, John suddenly recognized the root of his condition. Behind the worry was a compulsion *to be in control*. Because he was a very capable man, John could usually satisfy this impulse. But when circumstances seemed to be unfolding on their own, beyond his grasp, he felt forced into a crisis. In this case the crisis proved to be an opportunity for a breakthrough, and in the quiet hours of early morning he realized the choice his situation offered him. One option was to worry and fret over circumstances beyond his immediate control; the other was to learn how to let go, to release those concerns and trust that a higher power was able and willing to help. He also had to trust himself to handle details as they arose day by day.

When the sun finally dawned into a clear morning, John felt a new peacefulness. Everything would be all right. He was no longer worried.

He had made a discovery that morning. For him, worry was rooted in fear. Furthermore, that fear was rooted in doubt—doubt in himself and doubt in his Creator. In 1933 Cayce gave a similar explanation to a woman who asked why she was plagued with so much worrying. His answer was straightforward and clear: The root cause was doubt. If doubt creeps in, he warned, it becomes the father of fear. Fear, then, is the beginning of faltering. And faltering creates dis-ease throughout the soul and mental body.

How to Overcome Worry

As we stated earlier, worry is born of fear. And fear, in turn, is generated from doubt. This formula may sound intriguing, but exactly how can it help us surmount worry? On the surface, doubt seems as impossible to control as worry, but if we look more carefully, the two concerns actually point in opposite directions.

When you ask yourself, "About what am I worried?" the question focuses your mind on your problems. "I am worried about my job, my health, my marriage. . . ." But look what happens when you ask, "What do I doubt?" You might reply to yourself, "I doubt my talents." Yet implicit in that statement is the recognition that you *do* have talents, even if you currently question their impact. Or you might say, "I doubt the love and concern of God." Even this form of doubting recognizes the possibility of a loving Creator.

In a sense, your area of doubt "feeds" your fear and worry. If you doubt your ability to swim, you may fear deep water. If you doubt your sense of balance, you may fear high places. Therefore, fear is overcome by replacing doubt with faith. Doubt is simply a lack of faith, in the same way that darkness is the absence of light. Faith fills in doubt as light fills up darkness. When doubt is replaced by faith, fear and worry dissolve naturally. Therefore, worry in any direction can be eradicated by faith.

What is faith? To many people, faith is just a term they've heard preached at them; it has little or no meaning. To others, faith means accepting someone else's ideas without question. But the faith that heals doubt is something different altogether. That kind of faith is life-giving, growing in the fertile soil of personal experience and common sense.

Faith is different from belief. Belief is accepting something because of reasons; faith is trusting something without reservation because of experience. For example, you can believe that a cane will support your weight, based on an examination of the cane and common sense. But you have faith in the cane only if you're willing to lean on it. Faith develops out of experience. At first you may have only a little faith in the cane, so you lean on it with only part of your weight. However, as the cane supports you successfully, your faith in it grows. In the same way, you can build faith in God's help and support for any area of your life that is plagued with doubt, fear, and worry.

How to Change the Worry Habit

A woman asked Cayce whether she had any bad habits. In her reading he responded in the negative, then added: "Except worrying." Most of us probably wouldn't consider worrying a bad habit, but it certainly can be. Mental attitudes are as subject to habit as the way you comb your hair or brush your teeth. But habits (even the habit of worrying) can change. Bad habits can be replaced with new, healthier habits. Here are six ways you can transform the habit of worrying:

1. Observe Yourself Worrying

In the story we mentioned earlier, John's first step in conquering his habit was to recognize what he was doing. Until you realize that your worrying habit is directing your thinking, you won't be able to do anything about it. You need to recognize worry when it visits you. You can say to yourself, I know this feeling. It's worry, and I don't need it. Once you know what it is, you can take steps to deal with it.

2. Feed Your Mind New Thoughts

Cayce himself was a notorious worrier. In September 1925 he had just moved his entire family to the desolate, windswept village of Virginia Beach. They were isolated strangers in their new community. Their livelihood depended solely on the patronage of a New York stockbroker who had paid for their move. Cayce was so beset with worries that his health was failing. He gave himself a reading, asking for advice. The response was brief and to the point: Leave off worrying. When his wife, Gertrude (who was conducting the reading), asked how he might do that, the reading simply said to fill the mind with something else.

Other people plagued with worrying received more specific advice from Cayce. To one woman he suggested reading certain passages from the Bible that would reassure her when she began to doubt God's protection. In particular he recommended that she read and remember the words of Jesus: ''Who of you by worrying can add a single hour to his life? And why do you worry about clothes? See how the lilies of the field grow. They do not labor or spin. Yet I tell you that not even Solomon in all his splendor was dressed like one of these'' (Matthew 6:27–29).

Often Cayce advised people to read the Gospel of John, Chapters 14–17, to train the mind to think in new directions. Any reading matter or verbal advice that helps replace doubt with faith and hope is beneficial. Just as you are careful to feed your body with healthful food, you must feed your mind with healthful thoughts.

3. Lose Your Worry in Concern for Others

Worry grows out of fear and doubt, both of which thrive on self-centeredness. The more we focus on our own concerns, the more isolated and helpless we feel. To replace doubt with faith, we can direct our concerns outward to others. But even then we may continue to worry: Am I doing a good job of helping? Why is it taking so long to see good results?

To relieve these worries, remember that God is in charge. Do what you can but leave the results to the Creator. The impact you make in helping others may not be immediately apparent. Again, you have to trust that your efforts count, even when it doesn't look that way. Just remember that you are a cocreator with God. You and God are working together to make the world a better place. Trust yourself to do your part; trust your Partner to have the big picture.

4. Stay in the Present Moment

Most worrying tends to focus on the future—an imagined future that fabricates "what might happen." One effective way to disarm this kind of projection is to focus on living in the present moment. Do the best you can right now. Take every moment as it comes. Cayce gave such advice to a woman who was worried about the business where she worked, her son's schooling, and her daughter's social life. Cayce's reading quickly identified her unhealthy tendency toward worrying. At one point he told her that worry is simply each individual's fear of tomorrow. But he assured her that we do not live more than one hour, even *one minute*, at a time.

5. Never Worry When You Can Pray

This was the advice given most frequently in the readings for worry. The most powerful antidote for worry is prayer. Ultimately it is the power of prayer that fills the void of doubt.

Many people are easily confused about prayer. They think prayer exclusively means begging God to provide some possession or service. But real prayer is much more than petition. It is establishing a meaningful *relationship with God*. Just as we have many kinds of interaction with friends and associates, we also have many dimensions of interaction with God. Each could be considered a kind of prayer.

One type is called confessional prayer. But confession here doesn't necessarily mean offering up a litany of your sins. It can mean an honest communication with God. You recognize for yourself—and then articulate to a higher power—your feelings, attitudes, and problems. A prayer of confession means stripping away the masks that you wear in your other relationships. It is approaching the Creator "just as you are." This sort of honesty in prayer allows you to feel God's acceptance and support, something you can trust. That trust will dissolve doubt just as warm water melts ice.

Another kind of prayer is thanksgiving. We may be quick to turn to prayer in times of crisis, but when life is going smoothly we often forget to give thanks for our blessings. This is one way to cultivate an attitude of gratitude. By appreciating the good that has come into your life, you build trust in God. No doubt you have much for which you are grateful, yet it's easy to focus instead on your worries. Of course, when you're really troubled about something, it's harder to recall and appreciate your blessings. That's why it's important to have already cultivated the *habit* of thanksgiving. For example, remember to say a prayer of thanks every day, such as before a meal or at bedtime. The actual time of day isn't as important as the positive habit of being appreciative. This builds faith.

Petition is probably the most familiar form of prayer. The question we face is *how* and *for what* we can ask and expect to get results. The nature of petitionary prayer seems paradoxical. On the one hand the Bible, the Cayce readings, and most religious traditions encourage us to ask for things in prayer. In addition, Jesus says repeatedly that whatever we ask in his name will be given (John 14–17)! But the other side of the coin is that with this kind of encouragement we can easily turn Jesus into a kind of bottled-up genie; all we have to do is rub the lamp, say the name, and we get our heart's desires.

Obviously it doesn't work that way. Perhaps "asking in his name" means having desires that are in keeping with the ideals and purposes Jesus taught and demonstrated. "In his name," then, means to be motivated by desires of love and compassion. Worry can be dispelled by this kind of petitionary prayer because we're asking for whatever is best and trusting that God knows what that is for every situation.

A final type of prayer is rooted in the emotion of wonder, the magical feeling so easily lost after childhood that evokes awe and humility. It is called praise.

Many people fail to include praise in their prayers because they don't want to sound artificial. Behind our own words, we suspect, may run an unconscious motivation: "I'll praise you so you'll do something for me." Of course, hypocritical praise, whether it's directed toward another person or toward the Creator, is ineffective. But genuine praise is not an act born of logical decisions or manipulative motivations. It's an automatic response to the experience of awe and amazement. Einstein identified the experience of wonder as the foundation of all art, science, and religion. Genuine praise is an expression of an altered state of consciousness. In fact, we can think of every form of prayer—confession, thanksgiving, petition, and praise—as a heightened state of awareness. Through prayer we awaken to the profound mysteries of life and of God. Doubt is lifted, and worries diminish.

6. Do Something

The worst part of worrying is that it paralyzes. When you're worried about the future, you probably aren't doing anything about it. Prayer is something you can always do to replace worry, but you can also *act*. Sometimes almost any physical activity will help you shake off worrying. One woman found that whenever she was beset with worries, she would clean the house or rearrange her furniture. In the fresh environment, she discovered new perspectives on whatever had been bothering her.

In 1937 a business manager came to Cayce for guidance. In a reading he asked for any special advice that would be helpful to him. With a touch of humor the reading told him to hold tight and not to worry so much. It advised him to worry just enough to keep busy.

We all have concerns; we all care about issues in life. It's important to care. But care and concern are not the same as worry. Worry is a type of fear, and fear is based in doubt. In Matthew 22, Jesus invited his disciples to take a stroll with him while he was walking on the water. Peter alone took him up on the invitation and actually walked a few miraculous steps on the water. But when he saw the wind he was afraid and, beginning to sink, cried out, "Lord, save me!" Immediately Jesus reached out his hand and caught him. "You of little faith," he said, "why did you doubt?"

We all feel at times as if we were sinking into the waves, but if we learn to trust the helping hand, we needn't worry.

EXERCISE

As a daily discipline for at least a week, take time for prayer. Some days it may be for only a minute or two; on other occasions it may be for more lengthy periods. Experiment with the four types of prayer:

- *Confession:* Recognizing and admitting, without guilty feelings, the current state of your life
- *Thanksgiving:* Expressing appreciation for the blessings of your life
- *Petition:* Out of the spirit of your highest ideal, asking for what you feel you need

- *Praise:* Communicating the wonder and awe you feel when you consider the Creator

By the end of the week notice whether you can observe any changes in the amount of time and energy you spend on worrying.

PRINCIPLE #22

There Is Power in a Person's Name

Juliet, falling in love with Romeo, muses from her balcony, "What's in a name? that which we call a rose, by any other name would smell as sweet." Yet Shakespeare's play progresses to its tragic end precisely because the two young lovers have last names that entangle them in a family feud. Sometimes names *do* count.

Have you ever thought about your own name? What does it mean? Has it shaped your character in any way? Or do you think a name is just a convenience, a way of holding your place in an alphabetical line? Have you ever changed or wanted to change your name?

The Cayce readings placed an unusual value on names. In one instance a woman asked for advice on how to save her faltering marriage. One of her questions addressed the possibility of a name change. She had never liked her name and wondered if a change for both her and her husband would help their relationship. Cayce disagreed, suggesting they make no change because their very names were significant of what they had to meet in each other.

At other times, however, Cayce recommended that people might *benefit* from such a change. Once, as he was beginning a reading for a man in a distant city, he repeated the recipient's name and address (as was customary), then he inserted curiously, "Should leave off the Albert." He then proceeded with the reading as usual. The implication was that a shift in how the man referred to himself would have a significant impact.

Cayce had a surprising amount to say about the importance

of a name. One's name could become an emblem of one's entire life experience, he stated. Occasionally individuals asked if they should change their names in order to improve their "number vibrations." This esoteric system, referred to as numerology, is a method of determining from a name the key numbers that are symbolically meaningful. Cayce often supported the idea of changing a name to stimulate new influences or "vibrations," but he frequently reminded the individual that the new name had to be personally significant. It wasn't enough just to play with letter combinations to get a desirable number vibration; one's name should carry a deeper and more profound meaning.

For example, some people were told to use a name that related to a past life. If the events in that life were especially constructive, using the name from that incarnation could encourage the development of the same abilities. In 1941 an eleven-month-old infant was given a reading that said he had been the famous Hungarian pianist and composer Franz Liszt. His parents were given two pieces of advice. One was to start him early on piano lessons, as his innate talents would blossom only if he were given proper training. The other was to give him the nickname Franz. Using this name, the child would draw more effectively on the musical talent he had developed as the composer Liszt. Sadly there is no indication that the boy ever developed this potential as he grew up.

As we mentioned earlier, names are also important for their symbolic meaning. Cayce told one woman that in a prehistoric incarnation in the Americas she had been called Alta, which could be translated to mean "new life." In that incarnation she had experienced a major spiritual awakening, a development symbolized by her name.

A man was told that during a life in prehistoric Egypt he had been a compiler and coordinator of spiritual wisdom from different cultures. His name then had been Duo-She-Dui, which (according to the reading) meant "the duo teaching," or teaching by comparing two sources. Again, the name summarized a very significant activity of that lifetime.

The theory of reincarnation may cause some confusion, however. If you've lived many lifetimes, then you've been addressed by many names. Are some of them more important than others? The best answer may lie in the explanation that even your soul carries a name of its own, something that distinguishes it from other souls.

The Signature of the Soul

Each soul is individual and has, in a sense, a name. Throughout your long journey toward spiritual development, you are "writing" your name by the choices you make in your actions and thoughts. In the Revelation of John, an angel of God makes this promise: "To him who conquers . . . I will give him a white stone and on the white stone is written a new name that no one knows except the one who receives it" (Revelation 2:17). This passage refers to the "soul name" that is being written at every moment in every decision you make. Your vast signature will eventually become the record of your return to God. The white stone symbolizes this ultimate victory, while the *name* symbolizes your sojourn as a soul. Because your journey is unique to you, your name will be yours alone as well.

Jesus touches on this same theme in the parable of the good shepherd (John 10:2–5). The sheep know their shepherd, who calls them each by name. In other words, we are not anonymous bubbles in a cosmic sea; rather, the Creative Force knows each of us *by name*. This is a very comforting thought.

The Bible is not the only place where names takes on eternal significance. Chiseled into the walls of the pyramids of Egypt are hieroglyphics, an ancient form of writing that documents the spiritual thought of humanity living around 2500 B.C. From these texts we have learned a great deal about the ancient Egyptians' view of immortality. They understood the human being to consist of several parts, labeled with terms such as *khat, ka, ba,* and *sekham.* One of the parts that survived in heaven was the individual's *ren,* or name. Therefore, in the tomb of Pharaoh Pepi we read, "Happy is Pepi, this with his *ren* [or name] liveth Pepi, this with his *ka* (or spiritual body)." In other words, part of Pharaoh Pepi's immortality was his name, which lived in heaven along with his spiritual body.

In a similar way the Cayce readings on prayer and meditation encourage us to use people's names when directing healing energy. At the end of a meditation session, as we take time to send prayer support to those in need, we can use an individual's name as a focal point of attention. The name, with its particular vibration, creates a kind of address in the spiritual realm.

Saved by a Name

Ancient Egyptian mythology offers an interesting parallel to later Christian and Buddhist thought. Consider, for example, the legend of Osiris, Egyptian symbol for resurrection. Osiris was a god who had been killed, torn apart by his opponent, and then scattered into pieces. Later in the mythic tale his body was reunited and, in this resurrected form, ushered into heaven. To the Egyptians, Osiris was lord and judge of the afterlife. It was the hope of every pharaoh (and perhaps every Egyptian) to live with Osiris in the land of bliss. To assure this, the rulers of Egypt coupled their own names, with that of Osiris; for example, in his pyramid texts Pepi is often called "Osiris Pepi." By this union of names, he hoped to assure for himself a seat in heaven.

In the Mahayana school of Buddhism (origins circa second century A.D.), the faithful strove to join Buddha in paradise. To achieve this, they had to observe five rules of conduct, one of which was to invoke the presence of the Blessed One by repeating his name. This name, which they believed was charged with power, made it possible for them to acquire the highest virtues and guarantee themselves a place in heaven.

Anyone who has read the New Testament carefully has noticed this same theme in relation to God. There is redemptive power in his name: "Everyone who calls on the name of the Lord shall be saved" (Romans 10:13).

So What's Your Name?

All of this may sound a bit esoteric when you try to apply it to your own name. Is there any connection between your cosmic soul name and the name on your driver's license? Yes. Like the grander names, your current personal name may help define both your individuality and your relationships. How does it do that? Through symbolic meaning.

One person was told in her Cayce reading to begin using her middle name, Millicent, instead of her accustomed first name. When she asked why, the reading told her to investigate the *meaning* of the name and indicated that it meant "one who ministers, one who gives, one who means much to others." In fact, Cayce was fairly accurate regarding that name. According to the dictionary, Millicent is a combination of Old High German words meaning "strong" and "work." For the woman in question, the new name would help inspire her to work and be strong in her service to others.

But what if you were unknowingly given a name that means something like "rotten scoundrel"? Does that mean that you are destined to be one since you carry the name? Not at all. One man asked in a reading whether he should change his name in order to improve his business. Cayce's advice was to the point: Rather than changing his name, the man should *make something* of the name he already had. In other words, your name carries symbolic power, but only when and if you *give* it that power. Therefore, you may have a name that inspires you in some way, or you may have a name that represents for you a challenge or a difficulty. Either way, the name has only the influence that you get from it.

Taking a New Name

Except for customary name changes related to marriage, most people go through life without ever changing their names. Others may have occasion to change their names several times. But seldom do people change them for no reason. There is something profound about taking on a new name. Usually something happens to a person—there's some change—and the new name comes to symbolize a fresh stage in life. For example, in Native American cultures, which understood the symbolic power of names, if a tribe member had a major experience, such as a vision, that individual might receive a new name.

In the 1930s poet-historian John G. Neihardt paid a visit to an Oglala Sioux holy man named Black Elk. According to Neihardt, this encounter changed his life forever. The two became fast friends and eventually coauthored a book documenting Black Elk's sacred vision as well as his life story. To commemorate this special friendship, Black Elk gave Neihardt a new name, one connected with an element in Black Elk's sacred vision: "Flaming Rainbow."

The Bible is filled with people whose names were changed after a profound spiritual experience. Both Abram and his wife Sarai received new names when they accepted God's promise of countless descendants. Renamed Abraham and Sarah, they lived out the rest of their years as new people. Jacob held his own in a wrestling match with an angel and won the name Israel. Saul was blinded by the light on his way to Damascus and changed his name to Paul. In a similar way, taking on a new name is often part of an initiation experience. In many religious traditions, initiates entering a devotional community either receive or choose a new name.

Name changes can also take place in a more informal way. A man remembered growing up in the mid-1950s and being called Ricky by his parents, siblings, and friends. As a boy, he had been very entertaining and "happy-go-lucky." He'd had a special knack for generating a chuckle whenever visitors were present. Yet as he grew older, he entered a time of inner searching. During this stage he felt the pain and drama of life more keenly than before. In this period he preferred to be addressed as Richard, as it seemed more in keeping with the intensity of his experiences. Later, when he approached age thirty, he settled on the name Rick. He had mellowed through the years, and once again his name change reflected his new state of mind.

In our culture, marriage has traditionally been a time for changing names. But until recently only the woman made that adjustment, taking her new husband's last name. However, as women have developed a greater sense of independence, this custom is altering. One woman may keep her original last name, while another may create a new one by joining her name with their husband's. Some couples have even ceremonially chosen an entirely new name to symbolize their married identity.

One woman faced with this array of choices told her prospective husband that she wanted to keep her own name after the marriage. The man, who held more traditional attitudes, was uncomfortable with the idea but honored her desire. He realized that by keeping her name she would retain an important symbol of her rightful individuality. They were married and spent ten years building a life together. The marriage flourished, and by their tenth anniversary they were planning to embark on the life-changing experience of parenthood. For their anniversary, the couple held a ceremony. As part of it, each wrote in secret a statement of rededication that was to be read at the observance. In the company of all their friends, the two were married again. In her prepared statement the woman announced to her husband and her community that to symbolize the union that they were hoping for in a child, she was now taking his name as her own. Again, a major transition in life was commemorated by a *personally meaningful* change of name.

Using the Power of Names

Have you ever felt the thrill of having your name remembered by someone you admire? You feel a tremendous sense of identity and validation when you are recognized by name. Or have you ever felt the gratification of writing your name on something you've painted, written, built, or otherwise created? That feeling of fulfillment is connected with our basic need to be recognized as individuals.

As our society becomes more and more mechanized and less personalized, retaining a sense of individuality becomes even more important. In this techno-social system of ours, we are identified by the various numbers assigned to us. Thus we are a social security number, a bank number, a credit card number. For each bill we pay, we are asked to include our account number. Yet it is precisely our sense of individuality that protects our society from lapsing into mindless mob consciousness.

We can help shape a positive future by recognizing the importance of each individual's name. Through remembering and honoring names, we remind ourselves and others of an important truth, expressed in the affirmation by Reverend Jesse Jackson: "I am somebody!"

Personal contact is strengthened through the use of names. The tone of any interpersonal exchange is fundamentally different when people address each other by name. You can experience this for yourself. Deliberately use a person's name when the two of you are talking. You can feel immediately the increased rapport.

Perhaps, like many people, you have difficulty remembering

names, especially those of casual acquaintances. There are two ways you can help yourself remember. The first is to associate the new name with one that is already familiar to you. For example, if you're introduced to a man named Jim, you might say to yourself, "Ah, Jim . . . just like Jim Kirk, captain of the starship *Enterprise*" or "Jim . . . just like Jim Kinney, my boyhood friend." This quick association may be extremely helpful.

Another way to remember a person's name is to make a conscious effort to use the name shortly after hearing it—and before you forget it. You might say, "Nice to meet you, Jim." And then, a few moments later, "Jim, what do you do for a living?"

The power of names in strengthening human contact can work the other way, too. Use your own name. For example, when you make a business call to a company or another impersonal organization, offer your name before you state your business. This often affects the entire tone of your phone call. Most people greatly appreciate relating on a name basis. They want to *be* recognized but also want to *recognize* others as unique individuals.

There is power in your name. By your name, you claim your individuality. There is no one else like you. Just as every snowflake is distinctive, you, too, are unique. What's more, the very Creator of the universe knows you as an individual— by name.

EXERCISE

This exercise focuses on counteracting some of the modern-day influences that promote anonymity, that diminish respect for each individual life. For a period of several days, make a concerted effort to honor people's names.

For example, pause and inwardly commit to memory the name of someone when you meet him for the first time. Use that person's name, if possible, in your initial conversation.

Reserve a few minutes every day during which you pray for people, the ones for whom you have special concern. Keep in mind that the name serves as the individual's "soul address."

Among new acquaintances *and* old friends, make a special attempt during these days to call people by name in conversation. Observe how the use of their names adds new vitality to everyday interactions.

Health Comes From Balancing Opposites

I'm fit as a fiddle. My car runs like a top. My thinking is as straight as an arrow. I'm tuned in to others' feelings. What do all these clichés have in common? They all employ images of symmetry and balance. Stringed instruments make music because the tension of each string is balanced by the resistance of the frame. A spinning top is a perfect example of balance created by harmonious movement. Arrows, rockets, and airplanes all have to be aerodynamically balanced in order to fly, and radios tune in stations by balancing parts in their structure to electronic waves.

Our metaphors demonstrate how important balance is in all areas of life. What's more, we hear the word *balance* almost everywhere. Most of us know the satisfaction of balancing a checkbook. We're learning to appreciate the sensitive balance of nature, and Congress is still promising a balanced budget.

Equilibrium is demonstrated in every aspect of creation. The elemental atom, for example, is a result of the delicate balance of the opposite forces of expansion and contraction. It seems that life itself is the result of many balanced polarities. To maintain a healthy human body, as both the Cayce readings and traditional medicine point out, several major polarities must be balanced. Cayce often identified one of the primary causes of illness as an imbalance of the body's two nervous systems, the central (cerebrospinal) and the autonomic. The cerebrospinal system, which relates especially to sensory perception as well as to voluntary movements, is used, for example, in the conscious control of the muscles involved in keyboarding on a computer or swinging a golf club. The autonomic nervous system regulates the automatic functions of the body, such as digestion and heartbeat. If these two systems are out of balance, major physical problems can result.

One man who had been diagnosed with multiple sclerosis requested a reading. Cayce identified the root cause of the problem as an imbalance in his body's metabolism. This disharmony in turn disturbed the balance of the two nervous systems, which created all his unhealthy symptoms: poor circulation, insomnia, psychoneuroses, arthritis, and hearing loss. The reading went on to suggest measures that would help restore equilibrium between the two nervous systems.

Another point of balance concerns two aspects of the autonomic nervous system: the sympathetic and the parasympathetic. The first initiates the bodily reactions we call excitement. If you're in a crowded movie theater, for example, and someone yells ''Fire!'' it is your sympathetic nervous system that triggers the flow of adrenaline in your body. The parasympathetic, on the other hand, prepares your body for rest, relaxation, and regeneration. When you're sleeping peacefully or are in deep meditation, the parasympathetic system is in command. Of course, life demands a balance of *both* excitation and relaxation; an imbalance in either direction may lead to serious problems.

The body's acid/alkaline balance is also an important contributor to systemic symmetry. Many of Cayce's dietary recommendations were formulated to achieve and maintain this polarity. Whenever food is metabolized by the digestive system, the result is a residue that is either slightly acidic or slightly alkaline. Cayce recommends a diet consisting of eighty percent alkaline-producing foods and twenty percent acid-producing foods.

As you can see, *balanced* in this case means right proportion, not a fifty-fifty split. Most fruits and vegetables produce an alkaline reaction in the body, while meat, starches, and sugar make the body acidic. As you might guess, most of us tend to overacidify our systems. When the body is chemically balanced, it enjoys much greater health and vitality.

The common cold is a tremendous irritation to many people, and it's interesting to note that Cayce once gave a special reading specifically about this malady. His reading proposed that either overacidity or overalkalinity in a body makes a cold more likely but that overacidity is the greater culprit. What about the folk wisdom that sudden shifts in temperature, such as getting chilled at night, can bring on this illness? Cayce commented that these temperature influences serve to "deplete the body balance," creating a state of disequilibrium in which the cold virus can thrive. To speed the body's natural process of overcoming a cold, the reading suggested the obvious steps of trying to re-create balance.

The Balance of Acceptance and Release

An equilibrium between assimilation and elimination is also crucial to physical health. In fact, this one aspect is in some ways so central to Cayce's philosophy that it gave rise to a humorous anecdote about a serious student of the material. According to the story, the man was trying to explain the central ideas found in Cayce's readings to a newly interested person. After struggling for some time to summarize the many concepts from the readings, he finally gave up, saying, "It all boils down to two things: past lives and eliminations!"

Indeed, the readings do place great significance on this aspect of physical health. All foods generate a certain amount of dross when they're digested, and those remnants can become poisonous to the body. Additional dross is generated when we burn the food's nutrients for energy. The body has four primary avenues for eliminating these poisons: the skin, kidneys, lungs, and intestinal tract. All four need to function well if a person is to stay healthy. When a body is operating normally, the assimilation of food and the elimination of waste are cooperating in a balanced system.

But assimilation and elimination are psychological and spiritual principles as well. In his book *Creative Meditation and Multi-Dimensional Experiences*, Lama Anagarika Govinda, the German-born Tibetan monk (lama), uses the elimination systems of the body as an analogy to a healthful approach to existence in general. He emphasizes the importance of learning to let go, claiming that to make life great, we must not try to hold on to any of its momentary elements. The functions of the human body demonstrate this by reflecting the laws of life. For example, if we try to hold on to something, whether it is air or food, it turns into poison. Govinda concludes: "Exhalation and elimination are as important as inhalation and the intake of food. Similarly the process of dying is as important for life as the process of being born."

Lama Govinda drew a very meaningful parallel between the physical body and the rest of human life. Just as our bodies need to let go of toxins and waste, we must also learn to release certain mental and emotional concerns. Undue attachment to possessions or even ideas disturbs our psychological health just as inadequate elimination poisons the body. The Cayce readings clearly support this perspective: a healthy life is a balance between acquisition and release.

The wisdom of maintaining this delicate balance is exquisitely expressed in the Greek myth of Minos, who contended with his brothers for the throne of Crete. Minos prayed to the sea god Poseidon for proof of his right to the throne in the form of a magnificent bull, which he vowed to sacrifice on the god's altar as soon as he was king. Poseidon accommodated Minos, delivering a beautiful white bull directly out of the sea. The magical bull won the throne for Minos, but once he was secure, Minos refused to give up the divine bull. Instead, he offered up a substitute in its place, thinking Poseidon wouldn't notice.

But Poseidon *did* notice and punished Minos by creating in his wife, Pasiphae, an unwholesome desire for the bull. The result of their unnatural consummation was the monstrous Minotaur, an offspring with a human body but the head and tail of a bull. Horrified, Minos hid the monster in an intricate maze, where it fed on innocent victims. Minos had failed to balance his receiving with an appropriate release, thereby upsetting the harmony of his existence. It is the same with us all—anything we hang on to selfishly will, in the end, poison us.

Cayce reaffirms this premise even in the case of the spiritual energy that comes to us through meditation. Before a meditation period is finished, we are encouraged to release the spiritual power it generates by way of healing prayer for others. If we don't do this, the very strength we've received can become destructive.

Psychic Compensation

Ancient myths often demonstrate astonishing insights into the nature and operation of the human psyche. In the Minos myth, the Minotaur is a powerful symbol of how something good can contaminate us through our refusal to release it. But in a broader sense the myth symbolizes the compensatory nature of the psyche itself.

Modern psychology could offer an interesting interpretation of the Minos story in a dream context. The Minotaur, for example, would symbolize qualities of the king's (dreamer's) own unconscious mind. In the story, Minos is hailed as a great leader, bringing peace and prosperity to Crete. He consciously sees in himself only the noblest human qualities. Yet lurking in the labyrinth of his unconscious is the Minotaur, symbolizing all the repressed animal drives and selfish desires that Minos refuses to acknowledge.

In *Modern Man in Search of a Soul*, Carl Jung clearly identifies this compensatory nature of human consciousness. The mind, he explains, seeks equilibrium just as the body does. The psyche is depicted as a self-regulating system that maintains symmetry. Every mental activity—an attitude, opinion, or emotion—that goes *too far* promptly and unavoidably calls forth a compensatory activity. According to Jung, normal metabolism as well as a normal psyche would be impossible without such a lawful action.

To illustrate this requirement for mental balance, Jung narrates an experience reported by one of his patients. The young man had dreamed that he saw his father recklessly driving a car. In the dream, the father eventually crashed it into a wall. The man then saw his father stagger out of the damaged car, obviously very drunk. The dream ended with the patient feeling very angry at his father's behavior.

Searching for the meaning of this dream, Jung asked the patient about his father's driving habits. The father was described as a moderate drinker and a careful driver. The dreamer, too, was a very light drinker and tended to be reasonably cautious when driving. Apparently the dream had nothing to do with literal driving habits or the intake of alcohol.

But when questioned more carefully about feelings toward

his father, the patient proclaimed the relationship to be extremely good. In fact, he admired his father greatly, even bordering on idolization. The nature of the relationship provided Jung with a key to the dream. The patient had such an *extreme* admiration for his father that it had become detrimental to his own growth and development. This psychological fact was understood by the dreamer's unconscious mind, which followed the law of compensation and produced an experience of the opposite extreme.

In the dream the father is being "put down" and cast in the most unadmirable situation. The dreamer's unconscious provided a negative attitude toward the father in order to help the young man toward his independence. Thus, the patient's unconscious was making an extreme statement to counterbalance an already existing extreme in his conscious attitude.

Cayce also identified this balancing activity in dreams, indicating that they sometimes portray the opposite of our experiences in waking life. For example, a New York businessman brought to Cayce a dream in which he was at his job on the New York Stock Exchange. He was interacting with his colleagues in a joking, smart-aleck fashion but at the end of the dream felt bad about acting that way. Cayce's interpretation was that the dream was an attempt to balance an extreme in the man's waking life; apparently his manner at work had become too staid, overly serious, and old-fashioned. The interpretation, therefore, was not to behave as he had in the dream but to find a point of balance *between* the extremes. Here again, balance was the key to health, this time psychological health.

The Law of Three Forces in Creation

Virtually all creation can be seen as the dynamic interplay of three factors: an initiating force, a counterforce, and a mediating force that links the first two. Gurdjieff employed this model when he described the process of inner development. Every time we take a positive step to start some new activity, he explained, we will quickly confront a counterforce that resists or reacts against our initiative. This can come in the form of circumstances in our outer life *or* as an inner impulse in our thoughts and feelings. We see this process most clearly with new disciplines or new ways of thinking that we are trying to adopt.

However, out of this tension between the first and second forces can come something new, a true opportunity for growth. For example, suppose you decide to stop drinking coffee. Immediately after making that decision, you will probably encounter some obstacles to your follow-through. You may discover that your spouse has brought home a new gourmet coffee as a special gift just for you. Or you may have a bout of insomnia that heightens your need for coffee to keep you alert at work. You may even dream about drinking coffee in great quantities. How can you respond to these contending forces?

According to Gurdjieff's model, the answer lies in a third force that links the other two. When that third force arises either from the personality self or from material life, then the resolution of the tension isn't likely to be very healthy. One force may win out over the other, probably through a kind of defeat that represses the intent and energy of the other. For example, in the coffee discipline you may end up abandoning your good intention to cut back on caffeine simply because life circumstances don't seem to cooperate. Or you may try to use repressive willpower to overcome the desire for coffee and win a hollow victory because the suppressed desires will express themselves elsewhere.

A better solution is possible, according to Gurdjieff, when that third force comes from the higher, more essential self, what Cayce called the individuality. In this case the third force can build a relationship between the two that is based on harmony and balance. The intent and energy of both first and second forces have a place. In the coffee-drinking example, you may find a way to reduce your requirement for caffeine gradually without resorting to suppression of needs.

This process is illustrated in the story of a woman who came to Cayce because she thought she was about to fail in the crash diet she had just initiated. One of her dreams had discouraged her and made her worry that her cravings were far from extinguished. In the dream she was sitting at a table full of pastries and other sweets. As she sat there, she was by her own description "just packing it in," gorging herself on all those desserts. The dream appeared to be the mirror opposite of her eating patterns over the previous few days.

In interpreting the dream, Cayce first pointed out its compensatory nature. In her waking life this woman had recently gone to an extreme, at least from the point of view of her body, which was used to a regular intake of sugar. Then, wisely, he pointed out that rather than allow the first two forces—suppression via the crash diet and overindulgence from habit patterns—to battle with and defeat each other, the woman should make use of a third force, one that allowed a place for both sides—an understanding that would create balance and lead gradually to lasting changes in her diet. Unexpected as it may have been to this woman, Cayce's advice was to start eating sweets again, but this time in moderation.

The Cosmic Balance

When Gurdjieff articulated this law of three forces, he restated principles that have been recognized in religions and myths since the beginning of recorded history. Take, for example, the oldest creation myth on record, the Sumerian tale of the huluppu tree. Translated from ancient cuneiform inscribed on clay tablets, the story tells of a cosmic confrontation. Enki, the god of wisdom, sets sail for the underworld, a domain ruled by the goddess Ereshkigal. A great battle ensues. Ereshkigal hurls hailstones at Enki's boat and sends the primal waters to devour his vessel as wolves and lions devour their prey. However, out of this chaos is born something new: a single tree, the huluppu tree. Eventually this tree is formed into the throne and bed of the goddess Inanna, bringer of civilization to Sumer.

Thousands of years later the Buddha declared that the way of enlightenment is the "middle path," a point of balance between gratification and abstinence. That middle path, he asserted, could be found only by a compassionate heart.

Centuries later Christians identified Jesus as the mediator who reconciled the gulf separating God from humanity. In a similar vein the Christian clairvoyant Rudolf Steiner described the Christ as a point of balance between two poles. In addition, he identified the two extremes that create evil, two detours that divert us from our spiritual destiny. One extreme he called the influence of Lucifer, a spiritual detour that leads a person toward *illusion*. This is the temptation to a kind of egotism that claims too much for oneself. Lucifer would encourage us to self-flattery and a belief that we are wiser and more enlightened than we really are. If we stray from the middle path and follow Lucifer, we retreat into a spiritual never-never land, abandoning earthly responsibilities. The opposite deviation Steiner called the influence of Ahriman (borrowing this name from an ancient Persian god of evil), a purely materialistic consciousness that invites the voice of *denial*. In urging us to trust only that which we can see and touch, Ahriman tries to negate any recognition of spiritual reality. Between these two extremes, Steiner places the Christ, who holds them at bay yet is capable of transforming them and harmonizing their energies into a creative balance.

Cayce offered a strikingly similar picture. He identified the one and only sin as the selfishness, manifested in two distinct ways—the illusion of self-aggrandizement (in which we think too much of ourselves) and the denial of our higher nature (in which we think too little of ourselves) that is inherent in self-indulgence. Furthermore, Cayce proposed a similar role for the Christ consciousness, suggesting that only in the Christ can there be a meeting point of the extremes.

Finding the Balance

Cayce also emphasized many other forms of balance: work and play, physical and mental activity, wakefulness and sleep. But the question naturally arises: How can you begin to *achieve* equilibrium in all these areas of life?

The first step is merely to recognize and appreciate the notion that balance is central to health, both physical and mental. Next is to be vigilant and honest in pointing out areas where you are experiencing *imbalances*. With that recognition comes the work of trying to correct these imbalances. Usually that effort requires patient persistence, along with an appreciation for the potential good offered by both sides of a polarity. For example, in Steiner's model of evil the Luciferic extreme offers tremendous gifts when the Christ is in command—gifts of beauty and art—while the Ahrimanic impulse can be transformed from cold denial into the gift of science.

Achieving equilibrium in life ultimately requires practice—persistence that creates greater sensitivity. You will become more sensitive to what it feels like to be *out* of balance. For example, high-wire circus performers maintain their equilibrium by being more discerning than the average person. They can do what most people can't because they sense the imbalance quickly and can compensate for it in time, whereas other people would notice too late and thus fall down.

When our physical bodies are balanced, we experience vitality. When our mental bodies are balanced, we think clearly. When our physical and mental bodies are balanced with each other, we're ready to fulfill the soul's purpose.

EXERCISE

Spend a day observing your life. Where do you find polar tensions? You may find some in the competing demands of life, such as in the struggle to maintain a family life *and* have a career outside the home. It may be found in the conflict between initiatives that you're trying to take and the forces of resistance (internal and external), for example, wanting to perform a task but finding difficulty with the time element.

From among the polarities that you've observed pick one for special attention. Then spend the next few days looking for ways to bring greater balance and harmony into that point of division. Remember that equilibrium won't always mean a fifty-fifty split of your resources. Strive for what seems to you to be the best type of balance.

PRINCIPLE #24

Grace Is Yours for the Asking

It's official. For several years running, "Amazing Grace"
has been voted America's favorite Christian hymn. "Amazing
grace, how sweet the sound that saved a wretch like me; I once
was lost but now I'm found, was blind but now I see."

It's not hard to understand why the song is so popular. Aside
from its lovely melody, it refers to an experience to which we
can all relate, regardless of our religion. It's the experience of
being rescued. Have you ever suffered with a vivid nightmare
and upon awakening gasped, "Thank God that was just a
dream"? If you have, you know the feeling of receiving grace,
of being rescued or saved from a bad situation.

Although rescue comes in many different forms, the word
grace is most commonly used in relation to God or gods and
usually refers to a direct intervention of divine influence into
human experience. The theater of ancient Greece often made
use of a god to magically resolve the human conflict dramatically unfolding on the stage. The producers would use a machine to introduce some deity just at the time when it looked
as if the condition were hopeless. The god would descend in
this machine and straighten out the situation. This convention
became so commonplace that it acquired a theatrical term still
used today: *deus ex machina,* or "god from a machine," which
refers to any resolution that seems artificially imposed at the
end of a drama.

Today many people understand grace in terms of a deus ex
machina. They look for some magical event to lift them out
of their troubles and restore proper order. You may have heard
the story about a man caught in a flash flood. He was devoutly

religious and was sure that God would save him. He scrambled to the roof of his house and waited for the divine hand of grace. As the water inched higher, a rescuer in a boat rowed by and offered him a seat. The stranded man politely declined saying, "No thanks. God will save me."

About an hour later, as the water rose above the eaves, another boater came by and offered assistance. Secure in his faith, he declined again: "No, I'm sure God will save me."

Two hours later he was clinging to his chimney as his feet dangled in the raging current. Just then a helicopter dropped a ladder to him, but he adamantly refused to climb aboard, believing that God was just testing his faith. Eventually the floodwaters washed him away, and he drowned. As his soul awakened at the pearly gates, he demanded an explanation from Saint Peter. "Why didn't you save me?" he scolded. Exasperated, Saint Peter replied, "We tried! We tried! We sent you two rowboats and a helicopter!"

The man in this story appears foolish because of his rigid expectations for the arrival of grace. But most of us can probably think of times when we looked similarly for divine intervention.

Of course, much of the discussion about grace these days is not about saving the body as much as it is about saving the soul. However, the reasoning and imagery are similar: "If I accept Jesus, then my soul is saved and I won't have to burn in hell." Here the soul is just a projected image of the body, and Jesus becomes the same type of external puppeteer god who descended in the ancient Greek plays to dispense justice and reward. Is this really what grace is all about?

Raising Up of Xerxes

One of the most intriguing topics in the Cayce material is their symbolic interpretation of the structures within the Great Pyramid. According to several readings, the pyramid's architecture symbolically represents the spiritual evolution of humanity. More specifically, the lengthy passageway known as the Grand Gallery that leads up toward the central room (the King's Chamber) is like a timeline predicting likely events in the centuries following its construction. Certain markings and structures correspond both to historical events and to thresholds of newly developing consciousness.

For example, Cayce identified an area in the Great Pyramid that predicted the birth of Jesus. However, he described that point in terms of a shift in consciousness, a change that he articulated with the enigmatic words "when there is the turning away from the raising up of Xerxes as a deliverer."

To understand this obscure reference, one needs to know biblical history. Xerxes was a Persian king descended from Cyrus the Great who had liberated the Jews from their bondage in Babylon. Xerxes figures largely in the Old Testament book of Esther, although there he is called Ahasuerus. In this exciting biblical story, Xerxes delivers the Jews of his kingdom from the wholesale slaughter intended by Haman, the archvillain of the story. In other words, Xerxes fulfills the role of deus ex machina: he suddenly saves the day when all seems lost.

So why did Cayce describe the advent of Jesus as the turning away from the raising up of Xerxes? Because Jesus represents a new understanding of deliverance. Grace, in this new perspective, doesn't descend as a god from a machine to pluck us from sticky wickets. Nor does it trickle down from high up the celestial corporate ladder. Grace takes on a new meaning through the life of Jesus, something that comes both from without *and* from within us.

The Words of a Lost Gospel

The Gospel of Thomas is a collection of sayings attributed to Jesus. Dating from the second century, fragments of this document written in Greek have been preserved. The entire text was discovered, along with other manuscripts, in 1948 in a region in Egypt known as Nag Hammadi. Many of the sayings in this book are also found in the official Gospels ("The harvest is great, but the laborers are few," for example, and "You see the mote in your brother's eye, but not the beam in your own eye").

However, along with the familiar sayings, there are others in which Jesus identifies himself with a mystical divine presence embedded in all of creation. "Split a piece of wood," he says, "and I am there. Lift up a stone, and you will find Me there." Later in the book his disciples ask him, "When will the Kingdom come?" His answer offers a new understanding of God's Kingdom. "It will not come by waiting for it," he says. "It will not be a matter of saying, 'Here it is.' Rather, the Kingdom of the Father is spread out upon the earth, and men do not see it."

Still other passages are similar to ones we already know and with which we are familiar, but here they are elaborated. For example, in the Gospel of Thomas Jesus says, "The Kingdom is inside you, and it is outside of you. When you come to know yourselves, then you will become known, and you will realize that it is you who are the sons of the Father."

Compared to the New Testament Gospels, the Gospel of Thomas is most similar in tone to the book of John. Both have a strong mystical character and describe the grace of Jesus in terms very different from the "beneficent dictator" image of Xerxes.

Grace as it's portrayed in these passages is revealed through a change in consciousness, an awakening to the presence of God in all of life. To experience grace is to see with new eyes; as the hymn affirms, "Once was blind but now I see." What do we experience through the eyes of grace? We see and feel the innate goodness of the Creator. We awaken to the truth that we are known and loved, personally, just as we are. This realization brings with it a sense of being found, of coming home again and reconnecting with the source of life. Through grace, we become aware that God is everywhere, in every condition and in every experience. Most of all, through grace we sense the continued wellspring of life within us. Grace is God's gift of life and healing, a gift that constantly rejuvenates us physically, mentally, and spiritually.

The Testimony of Anne Frank

On July 6, 1942, in Amsterdam, Holland, a thirteen-year-old girl named Anne Frank, together with her family, slipped into hiding to escape the Nazi persecution of the Jews. For twenty-five months Anne was one of eight people secreted in a few rooms above a canal street warehouse. Confinement, deprivation, and fear were their constant companions. Frayed nerves and family squabbles were routine. Finally, only months before the liberation of Holland, the group was discovered, and all but Anne's father perished in the Nazi death camps.

Where is God's grace in this story? Certainly there is no Xerxes figure who saved the day at its darkest hour. The innocent suffered and died at the hands of criminals. Nevertheless, grace can be found, flowing like an underground stream. During their hiding, Anne spent much of her time writing in her diary. That diary miraculously survived and has since been read by millions of people throughout the world. Through her own words, we discover in Anne a heart that is not only sensitive to the love of God but also indomitable in its hope for the future.

On March 7, 1944, Anne wrote concerning their hardships, "I've found that there is always some beauty left—in nature, sunshine, freedom, in yourself; these can all help you. Look at these things, then you find yourself again, and God, and then you regain your balance."

On July 15, less than a month before her capture, she wrote, "I can feel the sufferings of millions and yet, if I look up into the heavens, I think that it will all come out right, that this cruelty too will end, and that peace and tranquillity will return again."

In March 1945 Anne died of typhus in the concentration camp of Bergen-Belsen. Amazingly, a survivor lived to tell of her last moments, recalling that "she died peacefully, feeling that nothing bad was happening to her."

Anne's story is a moving testimony to the power of grace. Throughout the nightmare—to the very end—she was sustained by a spirit of hope and courage. What's more, the simple words she penned in her secret hideaway have touched human hearts throughout the world. She was the victor, after all.

Karma and Grace

During a metaphysical discussion with a young parishioner, a church minister commented, "I have trouble with the idea of reincarnation because it seems to minimize the importance of grace."

He had a point. Many people who embrace the idea of reincarnation see it as a kind of "bootstrap salvation." In other words, they consider that the purpose of life is undoing the bad karma they incurred in earlier lifetimes. Eventually, they believe, they will straighten out their problems and earn the right to enter heaven with a clean slate. Grace doesn't seem to fit into this picture.

The Cayce readings offered a different view of reincarnation. It is unquestionably one of the key elements in understanding spiritual life, yet it *doesn't* supplant grace. To see how grace fits in with reincarnation, we first need to comprehend the meaning of karma. One way is to view it as the deep memory of the soul. For example, a physical condition in this lifetime may be attributable to the soul's memory of something it did in a previous incarnation. Habit is another useful way of understanding how karma works. We are all quite familiar with the power of habit, whether or not we believe in reincarnation. The Cayce readings point out that karma is often the habitual patterns of thought and action that have been carried over from earlier lifetimes. Every parent will tell you that children exhibit individual personalities from the moment of birth. Where do these peculiarities originate?

Karma is simply our own invisible soul pattern. Some of our soul memories and habit patterns may be in alignment with God's purposes, while others (because of our selfish use of free will) are in conflict. What *is* grace? It is the opportunity to change our current soul design into one that is more in keeping with the nature of God. We can, in other words, be lifted up into a closer relationship with the Creator through the influence of grace.

A woman who received a reading from Cayce was told that she had been King Herod's wife in the days when Jesus walked the earth. In her current life she had many struggles, including financial hardships and a hatred of men. Being conversant in metaphysical subjects, she asked in the reading how to deal with her negative karmic patterns. Cayce's answer spoke not just to her but to all of us: The choice is yours, he said. Your life can be controlled by patterns you've created for yourself over many lifetimes. Or your life can come under the direction of the pattern created by the Christ. *He* is your karma, if you put your trust wholly in Him.

Who Is He?

The theology of the Cayce readings walked a fine line. On the one hand, it described a universal God of love who is concerned personally with every human being regardless of race, color, creed, or religion. But within that universal context, the readings identified the life, death, and resurrection of Jesus as not only historically true but of cosmic significance. By totally aligning his personal will with the will of the Creator, Jesus actualized a new threshold of at-one-ment with God. Because of this union, this extraordinary soul was even able to rematerialize his body after death.

What's more, *the soul pattern of oneness* that Jesus established continues today to influence the spiritual development of the entire human race. Once achieved, Jesus' reunion with God began to resonate out to every human soul. Individuals can resist the vibration and continue to live by their own karmic patterns. However, the Christ consciousness continues knocking on every human heart, converting those who are willing to a life of gentleness and compassion.

In this perspective, the grace of Jesus the Christ is not limited solely to members of the Christian faith. It is given freely to any human heart that allows itself to be shaped by the pattern of love and selflessness. Christ lives in such a heart, be it Jewish, Buddhist, Muslim, or pagan.

Grace in Action

Grace is much more accessible than we may realize. For example, to one man plagued by stress, Cayce promised that in a mere thirty to sixty seconds of meditation the man could contact inner strength and vitality. That's how accessible the grace of God is to us all!

Even though grace is given freely, we can receive it only as we offer it to others. Grace is the love of God that transforms us. But the alchemical process is not activated until love flows *through* us in compassion and concern for our fellow human beings. If we want to have grace, then we need to live gracefully in relation to others.

Slowly—perhaps over many lifetimes yet to come—we will participate in the transformation of ourselves and the entire human race. Certainly the process seems agonizingly long, but even in the harsh, seemingly unfair world of human experience, the power of love is evident. It no doubt takes profound courage to face the world's injustice with a gentle and forgiving heart;

one is tempted simply to run away. But as the proverb says, "A gentle answer turns away wrath." The following parable describes how grace can work its magic over time.

In a small country village Tom and his brother were falsely convicted of stealing a neighbor's sheep. As punishment, each was branded on the forehead with the initials *ST* to signify "sheep thief." Shunned by their friends and ridiculed by their neighbors, both brothers were devastated by the disgrace. Tom's brother eventually packed his belongings and moved to another village, hoping to escape the shame. But the brand on his forehead went with him, and soon his story was known and the whispering and slandering resumed. So the brother moved again and again from village to village, chased forever by a past he couldn't conceal.

Tom, however, stayed in his own community. At first, as he walked through the town, some people would cross the street to avoid him; others would deliberately cross his path to deliver a fresh dose of scorn. But Tom just continued with his life, nurturing with honor and care whatever work and social contact he found. Eventually the mockers grew weary, and Tom's disgrace was slowly forgotten as he proved himself again and again to be a man of gentle integrity.

Tom lived to an old age, becoming loved and respected as a wise elder in the community. The *ST* on his forehead blended easily with the lines of wisdom written on his kind face. Finally Tom died, and the whole village came to pay their last respects. As the throng dispersed from the cemetery, one villager turned to a friend and said, "By the way, what do you suppose that *ST* meant on old Tom's forehead?" The friend replied, "Gosh, I don't have any idea, unless it meant Saint Thomas."

EXERCISE

It's easy to get in a rut concerning the way you try to resolve a problem. This exercise focuses on shifting your expectations. Try meeting in a new way one especially difficult situation in your life. Rather than expect a deus ex machina (an outside influence that miraculously sets everything straight) to inter- vene and save the day, experience grace as an *inner event*.

One way to experience that shift is to do whatever you can to be forgiving and open. Then act gracefully in the situation. Be prepared to experience a new way of understanding the difficulty

Epilogue

Each of the twenty-four principles in this book is a challenge—and a promise. The challenge is to see life as a wonderful opportunity, in spite of the disheartening, frustrating situations we face every day. The promise is that the universe follows reliable laws, and once we start cooperating with those principles, we'll start seeing big changes in our lives.

Why are these keys to living—so many of which have remained esoteric teachings for centuries—now widely accessible through the work of people like Edgar Cayce? Perhaps it is because of the special time in which we live. The chance for personal growth and cocreativity is unprecedented.

A thousand years from now, as historians look back at the dawn of the twenty-first century, they'll have much to write about. But among all the extraordinary political, economic, and social events they'll note, one fact is sure to stand out: This was a time of tremendous opportunity—truly an exciting time in which to live.

What will you make of your unique opportunity to live in such an era? Some people will be content to drift with the currents and to allow events and conditions to shape their future. The fact that you've been reading this book suggests you're not that kind of person. No doubt you have the sense that your future is whatever you're willing to make of it.

Admittedly some conditions that will arise in the coming years are beyond your immediate control. But you can always determine how you will react and respond to even the most difficult situation. By meeting each day with a positive, hopeful spirit, you will shape a personal future that brings joy and a feeling of accomplishment.

Keep in mind that this is a *handbook*. It's designed to be a resource that you can return to frequently and easily. As your personal future unfolds, make use of it to reconnect with the powerful resources within your soul. Anytime you encounter a roadblock, turn to the table of contents of this book and scan the list of twenty-four principles. Most likely you'll recognize one or more that will help you turn the situation around.

Edgar Cayce's vision of the future was an immensely positive one. He foresaw hard times as we moved into the twenty-first century, but those problems were explained in the context of a hopeful view of what lay ahead. Much of his hope for humanity rested with his clairvoyant image of the citizens of our planet in the centuries to come: men and women who use their freedom and creativity to live together harmoniously. You have the chance right now to start living that vision, and the twenty-four principles in this book are a guide along that path.

The ARE Today

More than sixty years ago Edgar Cayce founded an organization to study and research the material from his readings. The Association for Research and Enlightenment (ARE) continued this work after Cayce's death in 1945 and is today far larger and more active than it was during Cayce's lifetime.

The ARE maintains many programs including a publishing division, educational conferences throughout the United States and Canada, more than a thousand study groups worldwide, and a unique sixty-thousand-volume library at its headquarters building and visitors center in Virginia Beach, Virginia. Those who choose to become members of the ARE are able to borrow copies of the readings on more than two hundred topics. They also receive *Venture Inward* magazine (with articles about holistic health, dream interpretation, psychic development, reincarnation, and dozens of related subjects), plus regular study lessons based on Cayce's readings.

To learn more about the ARE and its activities you can request a free information packet by writing: ARE, Box 595, Virginia Beach, VA 23451.

Both authors can also be contacted by writing to the same address.

Index